METAPHOR
and THINKING

The College Experience

Marc Belth

Edited by
Gerard T. Johansen

UNIVERSITY
PRESS OF
AMERICA

Lanham • New York • London

Copyright © 1993 by
University Press of America®, Inc.
4720 Boston Way
Lanham, Maryland 20706

3 Henrietta Street
London WC2E 8LU England

Library of Congress Cataloging-in-Publication Data

Belth, Marc.
Metaphor and thinking : the college experience / by Marc Belth,
edited by Gerard T. Johansen.
p.   cm.
Includes bibliographical references and index.
1. Thought and thinking—Study and teaching (Higher)—United States.
2. Metaphor.   3. Education, Higher—United States—Curricula.
I. Johansen, Gerard T.   II. Title.
LB2395.35.B45   1993   378.1'7—dc20   92–42157 CIP

ISBN 0–8191–9021–7 (pbk. : alk. paper)

The paper used in this publication meets the minimum requirements of
American National Standard for Information Sciences—Permanence
of Paper for Printed Library Materials, ANSI Z39.48–1984.

To Zoé and Joanne, two ladies who lovingly indulged
their husbands' restless energies for a
different view of education.

TABLE OF CONTENTS

4. METAPHORS: TYPES AND INTERNAL STRUCTURES

5. MODELS AND THEIR METAPHORIC BASIS IN THINKING

PREFACE

I first met Professor Marc Belth in July, 1971, as one of two dozen students in a unique graduate program at City University of New York at Queens College. Over a period of fourteen months (two summers with two semesters sandwiched between), we were introduced to Marc Belth's ideas regarding the creation of a discipline of education and the development and use of teaching models based on those ideas. At the time, I had no idea that those fourteen months would so completely alter my professional perspectives about education. Over the years, I kept in contact with Marc and was privileged to maintain an active correspondence which became a written tutorial as I applied his ideas to my junior high and high school science classes in a small, rural school in upstate New York. After some further graduate work at Cornell University, I moved to another school district closer to New York City. At the same time, Marc was meeting rather informally with other alumni of that same program from Queens College to determine the next step in the dissemination of his ideas. I was glad to join in the lively discussions that arose from his work with the Freshman Course in Thinking that forms the basis of this book. Unfortunately, his death in 1986 precluded continuing any formal work beyond our own individual spheres.

The tendency to exaggerate Marc's ideas, his wonderfully sharp mind, his ready wit, his almost renaissance attitude about all knowledge and all disciplines, his impatience with what usually passes for thinking must be avoided at all costs. No one would dismiss that more quickly than Marc. Indeed, his own sense of humor and his own sense of proportion prevented anyone from taking his ideas and turning them into the new panacea for education. Anyone who was acquainted with him realized that while he took his ideas very seriously, he did not, as someone once distinguished, take them all that somberly. Aware that his ideas had much merit, he also realized that not everyone was able or willing to accept the alternate view presented here and in his previous three works. As you read and study this book, this will become increasingly apparent.

This work will more than likely be unsettling to many. To see thinking as a skill that can be taught and learned has been an elusive goal of education since, I suppose, the first caveman showed his cavechild how to build a fire or make a spear, and then expected the cavechild to consider ways of doing these with greater ease and more efficiency. Since then, in our present educational settings, we have settled into some comfortable agreements from a host of models about what thinking is and how we should teach it. Some define thinking as problem solving; some see it as a series of increasingly more difficult cognitive steps; still others contend that we learn to think about concrete things first, and only later mature to levels where we can think about concepts. Those who question the arguments in this work probably will have settled into one or another of these concepts about thinking, and disregard the reflective view that Marc Belth presents.

Teachers in a specific discipline or students who aspire to be members of that discipline often believe that theirs is the most important discipline that should be taught. Science teachers, seeing how the United States has slipped in the world community in technology and science, recommend that students need more science and math. History teachers will fervently try to make the case that students need more history since it is a sense of that past that is lacking in our students. Art teachers will worry about an increasingly mechanized society in which we live and lobby for greater time with students to develop the "inner self," an appreciation of the aesthetic, to provide means so that creativity can be developed in their students.

It is an assumption of this work that thinking is the ubiquitous thread that is woven through all of our intellectual undertakings and that thinking produces a commonality of action and purpose in the sciences as well as the arts. Further, its intention is to develop perspectives by which we can step back from events and concepts and say, "See, that's how thinking makes sense of that event." Or, "Look at this theory of science or school of art and see why it was invented to give new meanings to these events." In other words, it is concerned less with the products of our thinking than with the thinking processes that were employed to create those products. Once the focus has shifted from the products of these disciplines to the processes that created them, we can provide ourselves with a newer, richer appreciation in our minds of how science, art, history, poetry, and all the disciplines are created.

I suppose that this book generates the belief that the mind of the artist (although they would *like* to think so) are not that much different from the mind of the scientist (although *they* would like to think so); that what separates each is not the activity of thinking, since both do it, but how their thinking creates and shapes the different realities of our existence.

What is different is what each thinks *about* and for what purpose in order to sort out the chaos of our experiences, whether those experiences exist in the external world, within our own minds or in the long history of human events. It is (again supposing) the difference between viewing the creation of our disciplines as a team sport, with each "player" carrying out his or her job at their "positions" as we play the "game of knowledge invention," as opposed to viewing these "games" as a host of different, individual "sports," with each following its own rules unfettered, perhaps even unaware, of the other players in other sports.

This work, however, was intended to show how thinking occurs, and how that thinking has produced the major disciplines that you will be introduced to in your time at college and the years beyond as you embark on your careers and your adult lives. It was also intended to show that all knowledge construction and use can be seen as the purposeful creation and use of metaphor as the central activity of the thinking act. In that sense, among all the disciplines, no one is any more valid than another; no one discipline is any more real than all the others. With this in mind, I suggest that the more fruitful, even playful, attitude to adopt is the moral of that fable about the emperor who had no clothes. If you remember that little story, you will recall that it was the child who was able to "see through" all the glitter and pomposity of the king and his cortege and expose the ruse that all attempted to perpetrate.

But that deals more with nose-tweaking and the more irreverent parts of this work. In a happier sense, this work is one of celebration; a celebration of the inventiveness, of the creativity, of the indomitable human intellect and courage to remake the world over and over. As such, this work is not some sterile dissection of theories and principles to find their undergirding of why one school about thinking is accepted as "true," while another is not. It does not reduce thinking to some formula or flow chart, with prescribed steps to follow. To be sure, it is irreverent; irreverent in the sense that it will show the lack of "absoluteness" or, as some would have it, "truth" among the disciplines. It is an examination of the disciplines and the process of thinking that guided their formations, but it is not done in a scornful way. Like the boy who exposed the nakedness of the emperor, no malice was intended then, and none is intended here.

To illustrate this point further, let me offer the following. After editing the manuscript, I approached the administration of my high school to offer a course based on the concepts that the manuscript explored. In retrospect, I could not help being amused as it was decided into which department this course would be placed, under which heading in the course catalogue it would be summarized. Since I teach in the science department and since it attempts to demythicize the thinking act, would it be listed there? Since it deals with matters of history, would it be offered as a social studies course? How about the arts? Without hard data and with the notion that all our disciplines are the result of our own creative thinking, should not it be classified along with literature and painting? Perhaps, because it cuts across all disciplines, it should have been given a department all its own. Imagine: a Department of Thinking! But I do not suppose that would be entirely acceptable to my colleagues who would have claimed that they teach thinking as well. Amusing dilemmas that demonstrate precisely what I have said above and what this book is all about.

I would be remiss if I did not mention those people who have made contributions to this work. Anything like this results from the thinking of several minds, and they need to be acknowledged. First, I wish to thank Zoé Belth, Marc's widow, whose tender nudging and constant support gave me the confidence to execute Marc's ideas to what I hope are their logical ends and to finally finish the book.

To Dr. Harold Friend of the New York City Schools, Drs. Laura and Richard Sgroi of the State University of New York at New Paltz, Ms. Gail Glow-Davis, retired from the Freeport Public Schools, and Ms. Elayne P. Bernstein, Coordinator of Language Arts in the Continuing Education Program at Queens College, for their review of the preliminary draft of the manuscript and their helpful comments. Prof. Bernice Goldmark, Sonoma State University, made dozens of very useful comments that helped clarify the text. Prof. Heidi Hayes Jacobs, Teachers College of Columbia University, guided me with encouragement and suggestions as I executed some initial experiments with these ideas and provided assistance in the engineering of the pedagogy for the course. To Mr. Charles Ovans, former Secretary of the British Columbia Teachers Federation (Vancouver), for his kind comments and designation as "kindred spirit."

To the administration, board of education and colleagues of the Katonah-Lewisboro Schools for their encouragement of my work. To Penni Gallo, Thomas O'Day, Peter Grabowski, and Margaret Masterjoseph who all helped a "computer illiterate" ready the manuscript for publication.

I must also acknowledge the following high school students who formed the first experimental group with these ideas. Their willingness to reexamine some conventions, their commitment to embrace some new ideas, their humor, and their patience with the inadeqacies of their teacher made them a great bunch of "guinea pigs" to teach: Lee Baron, Alix Berry, Laura Christian, Wendy Carroll, Michele Chang, Tiffany Conroy, Cory Cowles, Aoife Cox, Oliver Dettler, Stephen Dill, Jen Diforio, Franny Dowling, Maggie Moran, Jason Parsons, Cara Peterson, Elizabeth Phelps, Shane Reilly, Rebecca Roberts, Rebecca Satkowski, Tammy Soltesz, Chris Tiné, and Courtland Willman.

And finally to my wife, Joanne, who saw how important it was that Marc's work be finished as he intended, and allowed me a sabbatical from remodelling our home to finish what came to be called *The Book*. The limitations and inadequacies that this work has should not be a reflection on Marc Belth's ideas, but attributed to the failings of its editor to successfully capture, in its richest forms, the thinking that this man produced.

Gerard T. Johansen
Bethel, Connecticut
September, 1992

1.

AN INTRODUCTION

*"The aim of education should be to teach us rather how to think,
than what to think -- rather to improve our minds, so as to
enable us to think for ourselves, than to load our memories
with the thoughts of others."*

-- James Beattie

"We achieve community with metaphors and consensus."

-- Robert Fulghum

With this work I complete a series of four, whose purpose it has been to analyze the various elements in the process of education. In the first I pursued the conception of a discipline of education as field of study, in the hopes of moving it from its present state of folklore and romantic ambiguity to a field of analysis of what is logically entailed in the act of educating. In the second I addressed myself to the creation of teaching and curriculum models that would be consistent with a discipline of education. In the third I turned to the act of thinking, which is generally held to be a primary purpose of any educational undertaking. Now I finally turn attention to the structure of a curriculum which would at once be an element within a discipline of education, the substance of the teacher's activities, and the content within which thinking is developed in the learner. And with it, I suspect, I will have said all I am capable of saying about the total venture of the processes of educating.

There are, of course, numerous subtopics which might be explored, topics such as ethics in education, or the rights of children and of teachers within that process, of the role of society in the ongoing process; of freedom of access to education by this group or that, of the roots of intelligence in those who come to learn, and many others. Of these topics, many thoughtful scholars and researchers have spoken and, out of the context of this work, anything I might add would be personal and ad hoc.

Perhaps some comments on each may be made, unavoidably, as this work unfolds.   But I shall try to maintain the primary context, so that whatever passionate convictions I present will at least have the support of the logical structure of the process that is being worked out here.

Let me first make some general remarks which are rather more intuitive in nature than logically analyzed and presented. I think they are fair statements of the current scene of education. Their merit lies not so much in their provability as in the fact that they have the sound of truth and faithfulness with respect to evidence about them. And they do serve as the substance from which this work will be formed.

Knowledge, Curriculum and the Student

The curriculums which we introduce to children as the substance, form and purpose of what is to be learned at all levels of education are all constructed views of how the world runs -- what needs to be known about that world and what we will be called upon to do in order to be productive members of a society in the world. In such a view, the concern that education has for the discovery of new knowledge is a concern for filling in further empty spaces in our knowledge of the structure of the world.

All of this sounds clear and reasonable. If it is somewhat difficult to achieve, it nevertheless would appear to be the only way to go if one is concerned to prepare children to be effective members of the society into which they are born. The dilemma, of course, is demonstrating that the world does indeed have just that structure, that the knowledge of that structure is all that we ought to be concerned with, and that it is the only knowledge of the world that is possible: a true, indestructible basis on which new knowledge will have to be fitted. The fact is, however, that knowledge is not so much a *discovery* of the elements of the world, as it is a *construction* of an almost infinite range of possibilities, within which the raw data of reality is given some form by some inquirer who shows an inner consistency and outer faithfulness with respect to what can be observed and known. All this with one caveat: whatever knowledge is constructed, whatever claims can be made about events, this is not, or ever will be, the final imprint of what there is. The acceptance of one such structure over another necessarily closes the door to any other constructions, and makes any new constructions a threat to what we have been obliged to learn.

When people come to rely solely on those accepted structures, the consequences of this is the abandonment of the active process of thinking, the very process that produced these accepted structures in the first place.   How a scientist, an artist, a historian or a psychologist reached conclusions, what was allowed into the considerations and what was not allowed, what modes of reasoning were permitted and which were not, are all, in the end, omitted from the curriculums in our schools.   Only the distilled,purified, and some would even say sanitized, end products need be attended to.   Even when the active process of thinking is addressed, it is usually made subservient to the conclusions reached.

But here's the rub: relying on the prevailing knowledge of the so-called structures of the world seems to be the sanest approach to learning, to teaching, to education, and to life itself.   We need something firm to go on, and to transmit to the young in their growing.   The world of things will not go away.   Nor will their organizations, and what we know about them.   We cannot really begin the world all over again, any time we like.   We cannot break apart the structures of things into their irreducible elements and reconstruct them into new forms in the hope that they will be more functional, more serviceable, more fruitful than they are now.   The weight of centuries and human success are against it.   Except for one thing: that is just exactly what has always been done.   The weight of our own conventional beliefs may stand against it and the poverty of imagination in most of us may leave us unable to do that, but this reconstructing of the world for newer and unforeseen purposes is precisely what happens all the time.   And sometimes, the very dissolution of our most dependable structures, the failure of our most cherished knowledge leaves us no alternative but to stop at least trying to piece things together again or using a shoehorn to fit new events into our existing conventions, in the hope of avoiding the inevitable dissolution of these structures.   But what alternative is left to us if our original conventions with their original purposes no longer function as we once wished?   At some point the whole garden has to be dug up, the soil conditions deliberately altered, and a new lawn planted.   Nothing less than this will get rid of the crabgrass, other weeds, and the continuing degeneration of the soil.

Curriculums and Worlds to Be Made

How curious it is that at one and the same time we cling to the sacred structures we have inherited from the past and resist changes in them, we yet praise and cherish that originality which breaks apart prevailing structures in order to develop new structures of greater fruitfulness with deeper meanings and deeper beauty.   This too is the basic contention in the curriculums of the schools. On the one hand, we protect our prevailing forms and knowledge of them by transmitting them in full integrity to each new generation.   On the other, we are concerned with teaching children to think, and thus to break apart those very institutional forms in order to learn how to form new ones.

Consider this: we are the hunters, the explorers, the constructors of the universe in which we live. We are also among those elements of the universe that are explored, hunted, and constructed to perform the functions others have written for us. Other animals too are both hunters and hunted, but they are not explorers in the sense that humans are explorers, and they are not explored by other animals in the sense that we explore ourselves. And certainly, the careers and the functions of animals are not written out for them, crafted for them, by the deliberate inventions of other animals. That makes all the difference, a difference which finally reveals itself in the curriculums of the schools. We educate our children to be, in the present age, at once both actors in a drama written by others and the playwrights of new dramas that prescribe their actions and those of others.

The metaphor of drama can be illuminating for our purposes here. Most of us recognize a playwright or committee of playwrights as those formers of the cultural drama in which we play. We cannot deny that some among us find our greatest fulfillment in acting out the roles prescribed or written by others for us. Others, more visionary and restless in their mental energies, begin to play with the raw data of the world, taking them out of context in which they were originally found, and putting them together in newer ways, just to see the results in new functions. Consider, for example, how the ice cream cone was invented. Two vendors at the 1904 St. Louis Exposition found a need to rely on each other. One ran out of dishes; the other was enjoying less than satisfying ice cream sales. When brought together, they found that they could wrap the ice cream in the flat waffle and the famous ice cream cone was invented.

Still others are not content with the raw data as they find it, and wonder if there is not a way in which even new raw data might be brought into existence. One has only to look at the "cutting edges" of art, music, science, or technology to see examples of this.

The Role of Colleges

The ongoing debate over who should go to the various available schools, a debate which at times takes a rather innocuous form, but at others a very significant one, is predicated on a variety of distinctions implicitly made. Sometimes the distinctions refer to individuals and their supposed talents or intellectual potentials. More recently, the arguments focus on the economic values of going to academic schools and colleges. Here the dispute is cast in terms of monies to be spent against the salary one may confidently expect to earn on completion of some span of education. In this case, the demands made on the college are that it must organize its efforts to equip a student to be able to immediately put the newly learned skills to work in the earning of a living.

There are also those who defend attendance at college on different grounds. Those who go to college do so in the name of the larger conception of human development, beyond the specific skills to be learned and to be employed directly in the working world, for the sake of what is known as "broadening the mind." This is the classic position that has its roots in the liberal arts tradition. It is not enough to be merely educated and trained in one's chosen profession, but it is also important, indeed imperative, that one become schooled in all the various subject disciplines with the purpose of becoming a well-rounded person.

The attempt to resolve this argument by casting it into a context of intellectual potential leads to psychological and political paths, and these must be examined sooner or later. The second argument, that of the economic base of education, however, points up the dilemma of the curriculum in a poignant way. For here we come upon the unfortunate, but long-lived problem of the distinctions traditionally made between the academic world and the world of life, work, and daily experiences: the "world of gown" and the "world of town," as it were. This is one of our primary problems.

The prevailing vision of the academic world is one in which it is furnished with larger, more abstract universals and purities of intellect, of the perfection of conceptual structures. The workaday world is the world of immediacies, of imperfections, of partialities, of irrationality in strivings and perceptions.

What good is it to teach and to learn this world of universals, of perfections in the realms of academia when the world we live in bears only wisps of those perfections? Moreover, what we say about the insistence of holding to this odd dichotomy when we come to recognize that the world of ideas is, after all, the world created by human beings in quest of deeper understanding of the world of experiences? That every so-called "pure" academic discipline is created by human beings out of their experiences in the world of change and imperfection? Then the dichotomy dissolves, and the contradictions are recognized as so completely integrated that the one is grasped only in the terms which the others make available to us. Thus, where a dichotomy between the two realms appears, it can only be because the academic world, coming upon ideas in their isolated forms and having been bemused by them, have never concerned themselves with their origins, or their original intentions in the work of their inventors, and the purpose for their construction.

So far, three "givens" have been identified. First, knowledge is the formulated views of the world that have been constructed by humans for some purpose of making sense of how the world works. Second, the knowledge we have accumulated through our personal existence and through more formal endeavors produce the conventions that provide focus, efficiency, and economy to our existence. Third, the dilemma of college is that there are many who have roles there. And their views and those of the society in general may not always be harmonious.

An Initial Perspective

This book is offered as a textbook for a point of view which, quite obviously, is not universally held. Nevertheless, there is a sufficiently wide acceptance of its basic thesis to have made this writing more than just an individual preference of one author. At any rate, the subject itself warrants its effort.

Thinking is so acknowledged to be a private affair, yet it is analyzed and argued over in terms of what evidence is acceptable as proof of the act, that we have nothing but continuous debate over how it might be defined and therefore taught. Incredibly, what adds to the oddity is not that the definition of thinking is so vigorously debated, but that it is far more frequently just taken for granted. We think. What more can you say?

It is not true, however, when it comes to argument that any definition is as good as any other. This would be like saying that one dinner is as good as another. On one hand, this is so, since each meal could provide the necessary nutrients for basic health. On the other hand, if there is more we want from a dinner --- ambience, conversation, sensory pleasure, family togetherness --- any meal is not as good as any other. So too with thinking. Each definition of thinking recommends its own explanation and description of the act, along with prescriptions for nurturing its development in students, and which must be evaluated good or bad, adequate or inadequate relative to purposes, consequences, and results just as dinners are.

Out of the several years of experiment I have conducted in classes with college freshmen, I have come upon some views that I think (that word again!) are worthy of consideration by a wider audience. The broad stream of tentative agreements on the basis of a specific thesis which I will shortly introduce, is brought in almost casually and informally. The references at the end of the book, however, gives a cachet of its connection to the works of such people as Paul Ricoeur, Julian James, Gilbert Ryle, John Dewey, Richard Gregory, Nicholas Rischer, Douglas Hofstadter, T.S. Kuhn, Karl Popper, and N.R. Hanson. None would agree completely with all the turns and formulations presented here, but there is a "talking field" I share with each of these; some more specifically than others. I do not name these as a defense of this work, only in an effort to locate sources and directions of the stream in which my students and I have been swimming.

What is of concern in this work is a discussion of how we go about making sense of things in the world, and the complexity of using or inventing analogies based on the things of the world. The same kind of analysis can be applied to the concept of "truth," with the very same results, distressing at it may be. Tables, chairs, mountains, snow, and emotions, other objects and other events of this world are neither true nor false. But what *we* say about them can be true or false. Their meanings are either true or false, ambiguous or precise, accurate or flawed. So we do not find truth *in* the primary world of these objects and events that we experience, but only in the secondary world created in the statements that we make about that primary world.

Furthermore, when we come to recognize that no analogy is a perfect transference of what we see in the primary world into some aspect of the secondary world, the concept of truth gets even more debilitated. Some parts of the analogy are a good fit, but other aspects are weak. So no analogy is all true. Thus, the claim that such and such represents "true analogy" is inept -- evidence that, as we will show, thinking has stopped too soon and settled for a conclusion that further analysis will not support. For this reason alone, along with others that will be mentioned, the concept of a "true analogy" is as meaningless and as empty as the concept of a "perfect" table or "perfect" chair.

Our problem, rather, is to develop a harmonious conceptual relationship between the primary world of our experience and the secondary world in which we actually live our lives and act them out, with order, purpose, effectiveness and fruitfulness. In all this we discover, all too soon, that our primitive efforts are always in the direction of fitting ourselves into the inferred patterns of order we perceive in nature. Civilized humans go beyond this "naked" perception, by reshaping nature so that it conforms to and is in harmony with the ideas and images we have for our present, past, and future mode of living. In short, we are now demanding of nature that it cease being whimsical, capricious and unbridled, and take on the intelligence we impose upon it through our concepts.

For example, we know that water boils, and we have invented concepts such as "temperature," "boiling point," "liquid," and "gas" to explain and describe what is happening during this event. More often than not, however, water does not boil at the prescribed temperature we say it should. Rather than thrown up our hands and abandon our attempt to make sense of this, we invent new concepts ("air pressure" and "solute concentration") to harness the event into a form that we can indeed manage.

But whether, like the primitive, we try to bring ourselves into harmony with nature, or like the civilized human, we try to demand of nature that it be in harmony with our ideas, it is by means of analogy that either is achieved. In fact, seen from this point of view, perhaps primitive people are not so primitive after all, or civilized people all that different because of our so-called civilization. In any case, from this point of view the use of such concepts as "perfect" and "truth" turn out to be merely protective terms, devices for hiding from the demands of thinking, by falling back on well-entrenched memories of others, willed to us from their adventures into secondary worlds. In such happy myths or protective lies we all live.

When Thinking Begins

Thinking begins when a person attempts to transform something in the primary world into an effective concept in some secondary world. This is done by first transforming something in that primary world into a form of an analogy, which becomes, first, a model to work from, and second when it has proven to be successful, a convention by which others can be guided in their own transforming activities. Thinking ceases when these transformations become conventions that are so entrenched that they are the only way of seeing things, the only way of going about our lives. Now, conventions are the organized patterns of belief and behavior that direct our lives. How we speak, how we dress, how we eat, how we love or hate, how we fight wars and how we achieve peace are all based on some conventions that we have accepted as some underlying "truth." Can you think of any war that was not, at its basis, a conflict of conventions? I cannot. Can you think of any debate or argument that does not have competing conventions at stake? Consider the last arguments that you had with your parents? Your boyfriend or girlfriend? In each of these, there is an implied convention that dictates what you should believe, what you should do, how you should behave.

Thinking resumes when conventions are experienced as restrictive coercions and some new effort is made to alter the prevailing analogy that formed that convention. It is obvious that resistance to a prevailing, deeply held convention brings harsh responses from those who adhere to them. It is also clear, therefore, that thinking by its very nature is radical or dangerous and borders on anarchy. But when it is said of an unconventional person that she or he thinks differently, you can begin to see what the intention of that statement is. Thinking produces behavior that violates the ordinary. And this can be said of any thinking person, whether that person be an artist, scientist, philosopher, historian, carpenter, teacher, plumber, or electrician.

Conventions, we know, are difficult to overthrow when they are well-entrenched. But those same conventions are very easily made the basis on which and from which thinking takes place. Indeed, what else do we think about except the limitations, the restraints and the warrants of our conventions? But there is an interesting relationship of habitual functions between remembering and yearning for perfection as we resist changing our most cherished conventions, and protective device we call lying. All these are curious in what they reveal about the simple way of resisting the hard work of thinking. Nor is this behavior limited to a given age or a given occupation. College freshmen, in the early part of their educational venturing, are too often stubborn; evidence of the force that conventions have exercised over their behaviors, their expectations, what is acceptable and what is resisted. And, it should be noted, that this is not restricted to how students perceive the disciplines to which they are introduced in college. Ideas about their role in the world, their sexual relationships, world politics, even to the types of food they eat are all ultimately based on the conventions that they have accepted as some underlying "truth."

Every convention appears so ordinary, so much the natural way, that people respond to nature and to one another in the economy of their accepted conventions. This is why it is hard to see the analogies on which they rest and which give charter to their structures and their functions. But when finally asked the question, "What analogy forms the basis of that convention?" or "What is that convention's root metaphor?" we can realize that, what we thought was some innate or natural way of doing things, was only some structured beliefs that we have accepted as members of one group or another.

The preceding does not recommend that all conventions be dissolved and that at every moment, under every circumstance thinking must occur. How muddled our lives would become! We could not reach a stop light and decide, out of whim or perversity, that we should go through the red light. Nor can we look at that light and wonder anew what that red color means. As drivers we have accepted the convention of the red light as a symbol for stop, as we have also accepted the other rules of the road that can insure that our driving will be reasonably safe. Conventions afford us economy of existence, ways of dealing with the day to day rigors of living without re-encountering or reinventing the world every day. So conventions are the source of great comfort, even if this is at the expense of thought.

Let me examine a little more elaborate example of this to illustrate these points. Since we all come to believe it at some time or another, let me offer this: *School is like a minimum security prison.* From what we know of a minimum security prison comes the substance from which we describe in detail and explain to a degree of fullness what the school is like.

Briefly, all the students are inmates, sent there for or in anticipation of violation of social rules. School then is at once punishment and an institution for the alteration or modification of behavior. Rules of conduct are prescribed, levels of improvement in behavior are established, conduct is rewarded or punished, terms of incarceration are fixed, release (or graduation) time is fixed, and when reached, the inmate is let out into the world in the hopes that he or she has been properly socialized, can now earn a living, will not be a further burden to society, will carry forth its rules in the character of one's behavior, will participate in forwarding the growth of the whole of society on into later generations.

Does all this sound far-fetched? Probably. But only to those who see school as something other than a prison or, as I have said, as another convention. As a what, though? As an "incubator," as an ongoing "business," as a "moral institution," or as a "shopping mall"? Choose any of these, or any other that you fancy. Then follow out the structures that are part of the model you have chosen. In each context, the roles of students, teachers, administrators, family, school boards and governmental agencies can be pretty well defined, their expected relationships readily described, goals quite clear, ways of measuring output equally clear depending on the analogy used. When the analogy is narrow ("*School is a factory for the production of useful workers for the national interest*"), the measurement of the school's effectiveness is easily quantifiable. When the analogy is too broad and indefinable ("*School is like life itself*"), measurement of outcomes is difficult, if not impossible. How do we define "life itself"? Since life is generally intended to include all there is and all there will ever be, school must include "all there is, all there was, and all there will ever be" -- in the formed and forming, dissolving and evolving states that life takes on -- the character of education must be about as amorphous and as resistant to definition as life is.

What I have done here, then, about such conventions about education, schooling and its theoretical grounds, can be done with governmental structures, with "family" as an institution, with religion and its churches, with citizenship, with patterns of child-rearing, with habits of nourishment, and so on. If all this appears to be exotic, be assured that it probably is. Although the basic idea that thinking is bound up with analogizing (or as we shall see later, metaphorizing), it is not just a little curious that it is rarely taken seriously, or made an explicit part of the educational experiences we undertake for a large part of our lives. It is exotic to ask students that they turn their attention away from the collection of established conclusions in various fields of study and attend instead to the structured processes from which all those conclusions are derived. Nevertheless, all students find themselves being shaped, even determined by those very processes of analogizing without ever knowing that they are being formed that way.

It is this adherence to the belief that these conclusions come to us as a reservoir of absolute, fixed, and unarguable truths that stunts any thinking and prevents the inevitable abandonment of one analogy for another.

Thinking as Learnable

Another aspect to mention here in this introductory chapter, but will be explored with much greater care later, is the belief that thinking can be learned. There is nothing mystical or mysterious about it. One can learn to think more effectively, more fruitfully, with more humor and deeper meaning. Also, thinking can be improved in depth and breadth when we learn to create, use and test analogies. Although some will readily dismiss this and argue that thinking is inherent, bound to one's genetic code or a beautifully complex set of convolutions in the cerebrum, it seems to me to be more hopeful to see thinking as the development of a skill akin to driving a car, of hitting a baseball or of writing a research paper.

What will put off some people is the very nature of this work. Thinking about thinking sounds so, well, difficult. That should not dissuade you. What will make this work complicated is not the level of the discussions, but what the work is about. In abstraction, it is no more complicated than, say, the economist talking about "economic man." This is an abstract concept too. The difference is that in the past and in other classes, such abstractions are treated as concrete statements, offered as facts, to be memorized as facts. What we will be doing, and what makes the abstraction difficult, is that the abstractions are treated as what they are -- abstractions. Not only that, but we will be learning how the analysis of such abstractions takes place. Because they are not offered as facts to be memorized, but ideas to take apart, the work will seem sometimes very vague, always "up in the air," without a firm footing in reality. This may seem too much for the serious, fact-minded student. Even for those who relish the ambiguity in the discussion of ideas, what follows has been known to produce a fair measure of frustration. This stems primarily from never having to consider things at this level before. For many, then, these will be the sources of the difficulty of the work.

But when it is finished and it has worked, if it works at all, you will never again be trapped into silence by abstractions. You ought to be equipped to think by means of abstractions, and be able to stand against them, demanding that they serve you in the interests of greater clarity of meaning and of use. With this brief introduction of some of the major ideas that will be explored, let me now turn to an introduction of those whom you will meet in your first year of college.

2.

A CLUSTERING CALLED COLLEGE

It is never fair to make a statement of total condemnation of so complex a matter as high school education. Even in a small area, there are so many variations in the quality and quantity of high schools, that a summary praise or a summary condemnation is all too easily disprovable. Nevertheless, there are general characteristics of secondary education with which we are familiar. High school often offers a protected experience, in which students are being socialized and fit into a number of proper roles they are expected to play. There is a common language they must learn, acceptable behaviors which will enable them to remain members of an ongoing society, skills they must develop in order to perform assigned roles, values and beliefs they ought to be guided by in order to remain fruitfully functioning members of the whole. In short, it is an indoctrination process.

But the first year in college introduces the student to whole sets of alternatives that are often shattering. Although college is not intended to destroy socialization, it inevitably creates tension within a given society by introducing alternatives to it, committing itself to developing critical powers from which the student suddenly learns to stand back and make some comparative judgments about the very society which sustains both the high school and the college.

From High School to College

Another objective of high school, beyond indoctrination, has often been identified as the place where students are provided with the knowledge, from a variety of fields, which they will require and which will enable them to function in a contemporary society. College has a more disturbing objective. It has the objective of learning to think, to use knowledge for purposes that no classroom can ever completely anticipate, and to analyze that knowledge and its basic assumptions. Of course, if it is unfair to make generalizations about high school, it is no less unfair to make them about college. High schools are never as bad as generalizations say they are, and colleges are never as good as generalizations say they are. Moreover, the differences between objectives of the two are not always obvious or even present. Colleges too often simply adopt high school objectives for four more years without alteration. But the principle of the college objectives remains, even when it is not attempted or achieved. It is the absence of that effort that readily distinguishes colleges from one another, the good from the less than good.

It is not uncommon that colleges are referred to as clusters, and the word "clustering" refers to a collection of things which are random, and only have accidental commonalties. Now, this is an odd idea to used when describing a college, since, on the face of it, it would appear that all of its activities, all of its people, all of its supporters within and without, are integrated into a common commitment: the commitment to teach, to expand knowledge, to humanize the "subhuman," to advance literacy, to preserve the finest in a given culture, to survey the world for the contribution that it has made to the advancement of civilization. The trouble is that such statements are glittering, even pious commitments and promises to themselves and to prospective students, but do not give the slightest hint of what really is occurring on any given campus, in any given faculty, administration, student body, or any community where the college is located.

In spite of all the buildings that house its activities (the plant itself, the classrooms, the laboratories, the offices, the physical grounds) a college is primarily a collection of states of mind, states of mind that are actually or potentially in constant contradiction with one another. At one level, for instance, a college is a money-collecting organization that is always broke, no matter how rich it is. That is because colleges do not make money, they only spend it, and they are always thinking up ways to spend more. In fact, the greatness of such an institution depends on just how much it can spend, how much it is able to raise, beg or borrow from all sorts of sources, in order to add new buildings, hire more faculty, enroll more students (whose tuition, no matter how steep, never quite covers the costs of an education), support more conferences, travel, publications, special grants to its members, and so on. From this perspective, the primary functions of a college or a university seem to be business functions. Another unfair assessment? Perhaps, since we all know that colleges have the primary function to develop the minds that come to their august halls. But we cannot avoid the fact that colleges must be seen as businesses if they are to survive. While you may spend all your years in college without dealing directly with them, campuses do indeed have business managers and directors who must view the college in precisely this way.

Those in the Clusters

Let me briefly examine those who are part of the several elements that make up the college you are to attend. They include the administration, the faculty, the students, and the community. All, I will show you, have immediate and long range influences on your education.

What administration looks for is harmonious balance (a lack of disruption in its ongoing activities) and something called "steady productivity." It wants integrated organization and a large measure of uniformity in its operations.

The goal of the faculty, however, is very different. The nature of "professoring" is to think, to think differently, individually, and unfettered by administrative demands. Faculty are concerned with the states of knowledge in their own disciplines, and the states of minds in their students. Their job, apparently, is one of transformation: taking students from one level of development to a higher, broader, more sensitive awareness of the world of the past, the world of the present, and the worlds yet to be formed. These concerns of the faculty make them critical, impatient, intellectually aggressive and foster disdain for the status quo.

A third group with its own agenda is the students. They come to college with a wide-eyed purity that has almost nothing to do with either the obligations of the administration or the intentions of the faculty. First, there is a kind of natural awe that students bring with them. After all, those people in the front of the room all have advanced degrees. They are scholars. They have probably written books (a most impressive fact!). They are, for the most part, highly articulate, self-assured, and have august titles like "Professor." So the students come with an expectation that they are dwelling in regions of great and pure knowledge, and equally great moral high-mindedness. Such expectations cannot but create special problems for both administration and faculty. Faculty often respond to this attitude toward them by presenting themselves as even more high-minded and moral than they had ever intended. Knowing this, the administration sighs patiently, realizing it can do little to alter these expectations, tolerates what it considers to be youthful absurdities, and waits for the maturity of the senior class to moderate the threat. The students have high ideals, and demand that the faculty and college live up to and abide by them. However misguided, the faculty finds itself obliged to appear as noble as students envision them to be. So the sources of contradiction can be noted here too.

But these are not the only three sources for contradictions in the life of the college. There are levels of community and their expectations that intrude. In the widest sense, there is the national community that expects the colleges of the nation to produce graduates with a number of different, but interbalanced capacities. This national community wants the graduate to be able to earn a good living, to raise him/herself in the class status, to live in a better neighborhood, to pay more taxes, to have the secure life that a college education is supposed to promise. In addition, these graduates are expected to have the future of the culture in their charge. They must become the future leaders, the defenders of that culture and the nation, the searchers after new knowledge, creators of new skills and products, the artists and musicians upon which the growth of the culture and the nation rests.

At another level, the local community wants something different from its temporary residents. "Come downtown," they will say, "and spend your money. But leave your crazy ideas up there on the hill!" Upon your entrance to college, you will understand this all too readily and all too well, since it is a very unusual college town that embraces the very foment of ideas and ideals that colleges are intended to nurture.

Goals of Those in the Clusters

When you put the expectations and objectives of the faculty, administration, students, and the narrow and broad communities together into a single, ongoing activity such as a college, I think you can see the tensions which must necessarily develop, and which will constantly keep that institution trying to balance itself without yielding itself entirely to one or the other of the pressures placed upon it. What adds to the difficulty is that there is no single arbiter of these striving forces. In some miraculous way, they must balance each other by having the various forces maintain some semblance of reasonableness. Although there are long periods of seeming chaos and disruption in the ongoing life of the college, the fact remains that somehow this balance is generally maintained. This suggests that perhaps the college does indeed have a life of its own, free and clear of all the competing parties. This may sound like a reference to some spiritual force that dominates the activities, in some quasi-divine way. On the other hand, it may only be a reference to the fact that whatever specific ambitions of one group or another, the machinations of the competing forces, tradition has so gripped each of them that in the final analysis each is somehow reminded of what a college is supposed to be and to be about, and they are finally driven to respond to the concept of *university*. But no one seems to want to depend on that while the going is heavy and the conflicts are hot. Each demands autonomy, and the right to tell the others what they ought to be doing, and what they ought to stop doing -- usually accompanying it with the phrase: "Sound principles of education demand that ...." Curiously, though, no one either remembers or ever quite knows what "sound education" means!

What must be kept in mind is that there is no malice intended by the conflicting groups. Each is perfectly sincere and honorable about what it wants, what it says, and what it is striving for. The trouble lies not in deception or deviousness. Rather it lies in the fact that there are genuine differences in the objectives to be sought by each group. When each group's objectives are isolated and examined individually, we discover a narrow and restrictive view of what a college should be. But when the objectives of all the groups are taken together, that hopefully produces the harmony that should be college. So it is in all honesty that each group pursues its objectives, with as much talent and cleverness that it can. The paradox is found in this, however: that to the degree that each of the groups is successful in meeting its own objectives, the deeper become the conflicts and the contradictions among the groups. Thus, if anyone comes to college with the expectations of spending a serene four or more years in quiet contemplation and intellectual pursuits that will strengthen the character and the mind, free from the tensions of the irrational world outside the campus, he or she had better be disabused in a fat hurry! College is not like that at all. If ever it gets to be that way or begins to seem to be getting that way, you had better look about you and try to find out what you have been overlooking. Either that or plan to transfer! College is not intended, nor has it ever been, to be a way to avoid the world, no matter what you may have heard about the "four happiest years of your life."

Nevertheless, there is another point to be made about all of these different levels of concern by which we identify the life that surrounds you in college. These different levels are not singular, or uniform or cohesive. In other words, they are not monolithic. In the midst of each level there are different, often intensely held views, about the responsibility each is supposed to carry. Trustees argue with one another, administrators dispute one another, students come with different expectations and different visions of what they mean to get out of college. Above all, among the faculty, the conception of what they are about and how they ought to go about doing what they are invested with doing, is as different as any two scholars might differ about the primary value of their own lives. All of which deepens the potential for turbulence for the student. And there is little comforting guidance to be given to anyone as to how best to go about getting the most out of your four years to come. No comfort, that is, but to suggest that you become increasingly alert to all these struggles and disputes, those contradictions and differences, and enjoy the very fact of the conflicts and the variety of visions you will be encountering.

What I have to say about faculty, about the professors who will be conducting your classes and, in one way or another, determining what your college life will turn out to be, whom you will remember, sometimes vividly, sometimes vaguely, more often not at all, is only a sub-theme of this work. The major theme will be to instruct you on how to protect yourself against the powers that they inevitably exert over you. This is the irreverent part. The serious part is telling you how their thinking produces the disciplines which we will be exposed to in your years in college. Although all of the groups identified do indeed affect the life of the college, those whose effects are most immediate for the student are the people who stand at the head of the room, or at the laboratory tables, the blackboards, the lecture halls, or the lecterns. What you hear about the world, its workings and meanings and how it is to be understood, come from there and them.

It is said, with much justification, that the quality of a college comes first from the faculty, and secondly, from the students who graduate and go on to richer achievements. The influences of the trustees and community groups are powerful, but noticeable only in the patterns of external requirements which keep the school functioning, and which sometimes impose limits on what students and faculty can do. Sometimes these groups join in a concerted effort to free the faculty and the students from outside intrusion that would prohibit free inquiry. Sometimes, depending on the charter that the college is predicated upon, both trustees and communities become the sole determinants of the life of the college and its resident faculty and students. You will discover soon enough the kind of college in which you are enrolled.

It should be clear by this time that college life is a complete world in itself, and mostly disconnected from the world around it. The college is designed to foster in its young minds such skills and wisdom that they will be assured of becoming smashing successes in that disconnected outside world. There will be many times when the demands and the tensions of that outside world will come barrelling onto the campus, and the walls between college and world will be breached. The world will be right there, on campus, in the classroom, in dormitories, in dining halls, on quads and in hallways.

College life is also intensely social. Clubs, sports, fraternities and sororities, dances, parties, dinners, lunches, relationships with the other sex, are as much a part of college life as anything that goes on in the organized classrooms and the planned curriculum. All of these activities make up parts of college life, and their consequences are as much a part of education as the specific studies you undertake. However, this book is not designed to advise anyone how to best take advantage of all these varied activities, to suggest what to become involved in and what to avoid, how to do this or that to achieve full value from your years in higher education. This is best left to those who have specialized in coming to grips with the social and the political dimensions of the very odd, peculiarly secluded world of college. The intention here is more narrow. For, whatever else may be happening during college years, its primary purpose is the development of *mind*. A concentration on this purpose helps keep all other tensions in balance.

College and "How the World Goes"

But with this very first, quite clear statement, the dilemma begins; for the nature of mind is one of our greatest puzzles, and it has been argued over without final resolution, for all the history of education and for all of history of humans. Imagine the size of this dilemma. The purpose of education is the development of something whose very nature no one agrees on, except to say: "Yes, that is its purpose." From that point, then, college studies can be most confusing, exasperating and contradictory, and will often lead students to pick out a leader, a guru if you will, some one or two professors who sound exceptionally reasonable. Generally, however, most students do not limit themselves in this way. Most students relish the disputes and the contradictions they hear in their classrooms, and although they quickly distinguish the deep professor from the shallow, the bright from the dull, the original from pedestrian, the serene from the overly dramatic, they do come to delight in quoting one against the other, just to hear how the professors respond. In this sense, the bright student is an absolute necessity for the professors who too easily believe their own reputations. Nothing will so humble a teacher as the intelligent student who quotes him in a larger context, and turns his brilliant comments against him.

Students come to college for all sorts of reasons, depending on the times and the pressures of the world outside. For some students in the 1960's, it was to become part of the antiwar movement or to avoid the draft. Presently, the primary objective appears to be the kind of preparation which will enable graduates to earn the kind of living, do the kind of work, live the kind of life that higher education is expected to prepare one for. So students arrive, even eager, to become competent in the tools, the technology, even the theories or concepts on which the modern tools depend. And the faculty in their particular fields are in agreement in this and do their best to fulfill the students' expectations.

But students also come to learn "how the world goes." And here, problems develop early. Whatever disagreements there may be about tools and technology, and their various proprieties, these are nothing compared to the disagreements among faculty as to "how the world goes." At the core of every study of history or sociology or anthropology or literature or philosophy, in theoretical studies of biology, physics, chemistry, economics, one comes upon different views of just how the world goes. For the fact is that there simply is not a single subject in a college curriculum that is not an arena of furious debate as to meaning and defensibility of its basic assumptions. At best what comes to be taught as standard in any subject is what most members of a given profession have decided to accept as standard, and, as such, the conventions of that field. Further, there is little assurance that the standard will remain so for any specific length of time. New evidence, at the most unexpected moments, from the most unforeseen sources, may bring about a minor or even a major change in the whole structure of any given subject or discipline. You don't have to look very hard to find many examples of this. The invention of relativistic physics, interpretive dance, cubism, even Freudian psychology, and so on, all began as a questioning of the basic assumptions and conventions within each of their respective fields.

Perhaps the first ideas that one ought to try to dispense with is the notion that there is a world to be talked about that is really well-organized, already known (though not by you), that truth is waiting to be disclosed to you in proper little portions, arranged for you into lectures, seminars, and courses. The greatest excitement to be encountered in college is the recognition that you are in the presence of the world that is constantly in the making, and that you may very well be part of the activity engaged in that making.

For the thesis of this book is just that: the world is always in the process of being made. What college is about, according to this thesis, is that one becomes part of that making by learning the skills, developing the powers, nurturing in oneself the courage to become a builder of the ideas that will make the world anew. Now, this making takes place by all sorts of means, the most certain of which is the developed capacity to reason, to make judgments, to be critical of what is said and what is read, to analyze, to evaluate. In short, to think. And learning to think is not an automatic affair. It does not just happen after a given period of time, or after reading a given number of books or hearing a given number of lectures. There is something much more, if I dare to say it so early in this work, "scientific" about this learning.[1] It needs to be much more directly considered, taught, and learned than has been the usual case in the past.

In any college or university there will be found on the faculty a remarkable mixture of gnostics, agnostics, committed believers, cynics, skeptics, nihilists, even intellectual anarchists, gentle people and vulgarians. Despite the fact that

---

[1]

The term "scientific" may make some of your wince. I hope not. By its use, I wish to imply that thinking can be taken out of the realm of mysticism and placed squarely where it should be, available and learnable by all those who wish to seriously consider its qualities, characteristics and purposes.

In any college or university there will be found on the faculty a remarkable mixture of gnostics, agnostics, committed believers, cynics, skeptics, nihilists, even intellectual anarchists, gentle people and vulgarians. Despite the fact that colleges and universities come wrapped in glittering but translucent raiments reflecting cool objectivity, it would be hard to discover any teacher who can long resist giving subtle or broad hints of the preferred world visions. However, what makes for real excitement in a class, even fun for those who have humor, is the fact that students have a chance to listen to those conflicting views and contradictions.

But apart from the pleasures that may be derived from hearing august and scholarly men and women disputing one another's views, each presenting formidably logical justifications for their own, and powerful arguments for rejecting others, something far more important might be happening. Since, in the face of contradictions, the knowledge you are asked to absorb turns out to be so unreliable, perhaps you have begun with the wrong assumptions about the purpose of education, especially higher education.

Consider this: it has been widely (though not unanimously, to be sure) argued that we cannot *know* what is not true. We may *believe* it, but we cannot know it. This would mean that any statement which we claim to know is an accurate description of some event, some thing in the world, something that we have or can experience. Disputes, then, about views among "those who know" are disputes over what is and what is not a true description of things in the world, of "the way the world goes." This is rather obvious. But if the wisest among us cannot always agree, what can we say about those of us who are just beginning to learn the ways of the world? How, when direct evidence is lacking, shall we decide who is right and who is not? Surely the personality of the teacher ought not to be the determinant, though, unfortunately, it too often is. Maybe then one of the most fundamental purposes of education ought to be to learn how to reason. But everyone says just that. We must realize, much as modern science has, that the world is unexpectedly erratic. Any knowledge that we can claim becomes only "probable knowledge" of the ways things go. And probable knowledge leads to the requirement of learning to think. For probability means that we would come prepared to learn how concepts are formed, how conceptual and physical tools are used, how conclusions are reached, how judgments are made and justified, how all of the tools of organizing judgements are to be handled. For knowledge apparently depends not only on perceiving the world's behavior, but also on the way in which we perceive the manner in which we make sense of our own existence, whether that existence is the external world or within the world of our own minds. This latter is not automatic or invariable. We must learn to perceive.

What I have said so far in this introduction deals in a very general way with the collegiate environment which surrounds you, the faculty, something about the uncertainty of the subjects you will be studying, and a little about the primary expectations regarding the overall outcomes to be sought. I have only hinted at the nature of the student. Each comes to school with a great many attitudes, beliefs, purposes, and dispositions. And few of these are just tentative. By the seventeenth or eighteenth year, the student, in spite of some uncertainties in some areas of life, possesses clusters of firm commitments and outlooks. As I have taken pains to point out, these commitments and convictions are rooted in the conventions that guide our very actions and beliefs. These are the foundations of the students' security. These conventions have been nurtured for the whole of the student's life, and they serve as a mooring for existence. Therefore, they give direction for exploration and for goals. The worst possible thing that can happen to a student in the first year of college is a shaking of these firm, even cement-hard foundations. Students will even adamantly say sometimes, "I didn't come to college to have my mind changed!" And yet we know that this is precisely what will happen as you encounter ideas you have never met before, beliefs that are completely foreign to you, people who come from worlds you did not even know existed, religions you know nothing about.

For most students, the shock of discovery will be accomplished by a feeling of excitement, even of satisfaction. But for a great many there will be a mounting sense of dismay, accompanied by a dreaded sense that the whole safe world is being washed away right under one's feet. Parents (not always), clergy (inevitably) will warn you against blandishments of new, terribly attractive, but dangerously seductive ideas. Students themselves, even without the stern guidance of their moral preceptors, will carry out these moral commitments and convictions, and have been known to denounce faculty for "irreverent" ideas, for espousing "destructive" doctrine. On the other hand, it is not unknown that a parent will pound the dinner table and shout: "You may be a college student, but here you are still our child! So shut up with your crazy ideas and eat your dinner!"

But this is college, university, you are entering, and the name "university" has relationships with the term "universal." It is expected to deal with all of the things that human beings have confronted, have argued about, have found out, everywhere, in all human times. Moreover, it is concerned not with just one person's explorations and findings, but with the explorations and findings of all people, of what others say of one's own conclusions. Still further, it seeks to deal with the faiths of all people, everywhere, in all times, those of all colors, all religions, all philosophies, all moral systems, as well as the whole range of views that give distinction to the various fields you will be studying in good time.

To come to school, then, with so firm a set of faiths, either religious or secular, as to what science is, or what poetry is, or what history is, or what psychology is, and what the truths are in each, and to be upset or to become angered over alien ideas, is to defeat the purposes of the university from the first moment.   What the student must nurture within him/herself is unbounded *courage*, the courage to listen with an open mind, to remember that what you may be hearing for the first time is the work of honorable people, as honorable as you yourselves are. All of them have their own beliefs, just as you do, with concerns for truth and honor and personal fulfillments that you yourselves have. To be so cautious as to guard against alien ideas, to filter them, or to block them out altogether, is simply evidence of an intellectual or even a moral lack of courage.   Such courage is replaced with dogma, which makes any further investigation of ideas not simply unnecessary, but positively heretical.   Yet history is full of heretics who have created not only new visions of the world, but new worlds altogether.

A second matter you must concentrate on deals with the *imagination*. Now this concept is not easily defined because its nature is not fully agreed upon by those who invoke it as a fundamental power. But this seems acceptable to all: imagination has much in common with courage. It takes courage to face the established order of things, with its established beliefs, and its established ways of behaving. It takes courage to look at alternatives, to listen to alternative ideas, and to invent newer alternatives not yet conceived by others. The courage to say something different and new depends on the courage to exercise one's imagination. When your capacity to imagine what is not yet, or could not possibly be, as things seem to stand at the moment, is blocked off by some devoutly held convictions that you bring into your classes with you, as some iron shield of protection against the contamination from the pagans and the heretics about you, then you might as well not have come in the first place. You would have done better to have stayed in the security of your tent in the desert, where other people and other minds pass at rare times, where the alien winds of strange ideas are heard only from safe distances, if they are ever heard at all.

Thinking and Reality

We come to college to learn how to think as others have thought and experienced, however vicariously, the moments of imagination and enlightenment of the faculty and their colleagues, both living and dead, that they discuss. Now there is a long standing tradition that holds that if we have learned enough facts, absorbed enough "truths," the capacity to think develops as a special bonus, a synergistic residue of learning all those facts and ideas. But thinking is an activity, a skill, and it can be and needs to be learned by direct and diligent attention. This view stands in direct contradiction to our tradition, for it also implies that in some way we can actually detect and directly improve the act of thinking.

The shift from learning facts and conclusions in different fields, to learning how to think, is far more dramatic, even devastating than would appear at first glance. It demands first of all, a shift on the part of the students, from a posture of passivity, of quiet absorption of what is laid out before them, to an active, even a dynamic posture.

But this is quite ahead of ourselves. We need to be aware first that we have as yet not discovered a way of getting inside the act itself in order to describe it so faithfully that anyone else who gets inside the act will come out of it and say, "Yes, that is a true description of what goes on when a person thinks." Not even neurologists have been able to effectively connect the behavior of brain chemicals with the actual appearance or production of conceptual activity. It is therefore reasonable to say that any statement about what constitutes thinking is a hypothesis. It becomes a recommendation or suggestion that says in effect, "Why not try thinking about thinking in these terms, as this kind of activity, or as involving these kinds of conceptual relationships?" If we do that, I am suggesting, we may form a definition of thinking that will enable us to do more with the concept than we have in the past. Every such recommendation, certainly at the outset, stands as good a chance of being acceptable as any other. It waits upon further exploration and analysis to discover which is more fruitful, which more fanciful, which more reliant upon testable evidence, and which gets us lost in curious kinds of mysticism. A certain amount of common sense experience is usually relied upon at the outset to make discriminations. In the long run, however, not even common sense will be sufficient to help us come to grips with this problem. Since we cannot see thinking going on, we can only respond to the products of thinking: a poem, a speech, a theory, a painting, a piece of music. At that point we can only infer backwards in order to say "that was good thinking."

I want to stress a point made just a moment ago. I said that we cannot see thinking when it is occurring. The importance of this is simply incalculable. Most of us now live in a world totally dominated by empirical demands and requirements. We seem only to believe what can be demonstrated, is visible, or has some immediate physical presence. When we talk about things, we want the opportunity to see what it is we are talking about. If we can neither see it nor have the promise of seeing it at some later time with more powerful instruments, we have learned to dismiss such statements as mythologies or as a return to some form of mysticism or simply articles of faith. To press the point even further, one of the most famous and respected of modern psychologists, B.F. Skinner, has written a book attempting to show that arguments about freedom and dignity are nothing more than the revival of an appeal to an old mythology in which emotional expressions are assumed to have concrete form, which of course they do not. This has proved to be shocking to many people. There was a Viennese philosopher who created the delightful aphorism, "Of that we cannot speak, say nothing." Meaning what? Meaning simply that if a thing does not have physical dimensions, cannot be weighed or measured, and does not displace space, it does not exist, and therefore, cannot be talked about. To attempt to do so is to summon up old ghosts, goblins, and other mystical powers that control the world no matter what we do, try to do or even think about.

There is, of course, a wonderful paradox in statements like these. To prove them to be true you would have to identify what does not exist and then, having identified it, in some undefined way, because it cannot be seen, show that it does not really exist. This is like the jealous soprano, hearing another soprano sing an E above high A, saying, "There is no such note!" Meaning that the note not only does not exist, it is purely superstition or myth. In all these cases, reality or existence has been defined by assumption, not by actual description. Now this statement contradicts itself.

The other comment to be made with respect to this view is equally simple. How untroubling the world would be if the only things we were ever permitted to talk about, to clarify, to argue over, would be the tangible or experiential things in the world. But then, there would never have been any science, any sociology, any psychology, or any subject at all which makes up collegiate studies. Some of you, of course, might be quite gratified with such a state of affairs, but in all fairness you must think of all the people, from time immemorial, it would have, and would now, put out of work. Your whole education would become an education of miscellaneous collections, a rhapsody, a clustering.

It would seem the better part of wisdom not to dismiss altogether that which does not have a tangible character in the explicit form stated above. We need, rather, to learn ways of talking about them. This is, after all, what the sciences, both natural and social, the humanities and the arts have been about throughout the length of human history. And this is what this section is now about. It is about the differences between statements that lend themselves to physical proof, and the statements whose purpose it is to organize and give conceptual meanings to empirical statements. But what does this have to do with thinking? If we understand that we cannot in any empirical way demonstrate what thinking is and that we cannot read any concreteness into pure concepts, we will save ourselves a great deal of mental and emotional confusion.

A Suggestion for a Definition of Thinking

A widely accepted definition of thinking today is that it is best understood as "problem solving," a term you have been introduced to in high school. Generally, this is further explained in the terms of ordinary events and situations. During a series of habitual activities, something intrudes to stop the action. Examine what the delay is, look for what was not expected, isolate the blockage, choose a path of action that would overcome that dilemma and then proceed again. This is what is called "thinking." More carefully stated, we locate a problem, we set forth the conditions which have produced it, we project a possible solution, we try out the recommendations for the solution, and if it does not work, we set up another possible solution based on what evidence we have before us as to the cause of the blockage, until action is going on again. At the end we note the series of steps we have taken, the problem which occurred, and the way we solved it; all this is a guidance for the possible recurrence of just this kind, or a similar kind of problem.

But all of this is too simple. It leaves open many questions. It appears too casual, too general a description. It does not give very precise directions for identifying problems, or for organizing the data involved in such problems, or for the logical sequence of procedures to be followed.

This is a good place to introduce what I consider to be a critical point of this work. In the very nature of the term, the unconscious is not observable in any actual or empirical sense. It can only be postulated, and postulated by means of an analogy. What this means is that if we use what we can observe as a guide for explaining what we cannot observe, then we can create an explanation for the unobservable. This, we will discover, in later examination of various subjects which we study, is what all of the sciences do, what the humanities and the arts do, what we do in common sense problems we face. If we treat what cannot be observed, yet suspect is going on, *as if* it were like what can be observed, we can mentally connect events that remain otherwise unconnected or disconnected. Of course, we must explain how to justify the *as if*, the applicability of the *as if* of the observable to the unobservable. This is no simple matter. If it is unobservable, how do we check for the correctness of the connection, constructed analogy? Must we? This will be discussed when I examine analogy in greater detail in the following chapters.

We are chased back to what appears to be a recurring question: the debate over what we ought to rely on as the ultimate test of validity in statements which we make. Is it true that "the heart knows reasons that the mind knows not of"? (Pascal) Are we born with certain kinds or bits of knowledge which we never need to learn, which we can never learn in direct experience (Plato)? Does some

God endow some of us with knowledge or genius which is denied to others (The scholastic tradition)? Or is our intelligence determined by random sequencing of the DNA code in our chromosomes (the "new" biological tradition)? How do we demonstrate any such insistences, other than by the utterly private and absurd conviction that because I believe it so intensely, it must be true? If we accept that kind of belief, are we not mistaken in the conviction that education is of value to all, no matter what the conditions of birth? More important, if we have no way of demonstrating such a view, we will also have no way of distinguishing between something we call innate knowledge from those things that we learn simply in the course of living.

I have raised just enough questions here to offer a suggestion. The question to be addressed here is not only which definition is the correct one, but what shall we accept as evidence for the better or the "less better" definition. And this brings us back momentarily to the matter of analogy. For if it comes to a matter of making choices about evidence that would explain observable outcomes, observable events have come to take a greater hold on our allegiance than faith in mysterious endowments. Whatever the weaknesses in religious concerns, in matters of human experience, being a Doubting Thomas has become accepted as the more potentially reasonable way to go.

My own view is, be sure you remember, as tentative and as much open to dispute as any other view of what thinking is: only what we experience is the best guide to explain what we cannot experience or measure directly. In this way, I persuade myself, I can go from what I know to what I do not yet know, but want to, through the connections I can make between experiences and experiences, concepts and concepts.

One final point to conclude this chapter. I intend to show that analogy is one type of *metaphor*, and like all of the other types which I will tell you about, it has certain forms, certain ways of functioning, and certain limitations. It is by means of analogy that we suggest that what can be observed, what can be demonstrated, what relationships are said to prevail among what is known can be transferred to a realm that we cannot observe. So, for example, the scientist who argues that unconscious thinking behaves or follows the same processes as conscious thinking, has offered us an analogy from what we might observe to describe and explain what we cannot. In this case, however, there is an obvious but odd dilemma: the thinking process we call conscious is no more observable than the unconscious. So a description of thinking as "problem solving" is itself non-empirical and metaphorical right from the beginning. And this metaphor is employed (to add confusion to mystery) metaphorically to describe and explain something else that we cannot observe, namely, unconscious thinking.

Summary

This chapter, then, has addressed itself to several things. I have identified what the student comes into college with, relative to beliefs and attitudes; of faculty and their range of manners, mannerisms, expectations and traits; of administration and community that function as governing agents in the cluster called college; and suggested the traditional views of what college is for. I have also suggested that the "development of mind," as a major goal of colleges, leaves much to be desired since no one can agree on what the nature of the mind is. The dilemma that this lack of definition produces requires us to shift our attention away from a definition of mind to a functional, workable definition of the thinking act. As I will show throughout this book, there is a common thread that can be woven through all the disciplines that you will encounter in all the courses that you will take during your college years. With that perspective, I concentrated on the central factor of the act of thinking, because all of the studies which comprise a college career are unified in this act. The clearer we are about this, the greater the possibility of real accomplishment in your work over the next several years, and even after. To this, the rest of the work is directed, in increasing critical detail.

3.

THE ROLE OF METAPHOR

IN THINKING

When novelists write stories or producers make movies of academic life, they revel in the lunacy that is so characteristic of it. It is an irresistible theme, whether the central characters are members of the faculty, the administration, the student body or the college town. See the movie *Animal House*, for instance, for a slap-stick and most irreverent depiction of college life. Examine the movie in light of the discussion in the last chapter and what will be said momentarily. What is celebrated is the gap between the purity of thought and the impurity of the striving for honors, grades, and conquests (sex and money always get into the stories). Educational institutions lend themselves to this. If they gave themselves over only to the purity of thought, then they would transform themselves into Herman Hesse's *Glass Bead Game*, a vacuum of noble sterility. If they gave themselves over only to the impurity of striving and conquest, the campus would become a battlefield of furious wills with bodies of destroyed egos lying all over the terrain.

We ought to be grateful for the lunatic tensions that keep campuses in motion. It makes great fiction, especially when it comes close to reality. What I must say here is something about the terrible conditions which are produced when teachers and students make dull the excitement of discovery, the joys of invention, or both. We should remember that it is in the educational venture that the exploration of worlds that are, that were, and that might be, takes place. Unfortunately, for the most part, these worlds are cut, divided, repackaged and merchandised like so many cold cuts that we are invited to select from. The serving platters are often decorated to make them appear more appetizing, and are accompanied by small entertainments which are designed to aid the digestion. This perspective begins with the conviction that students are a captive audience and must be amused or be destined to boredom altogether. The idea that it might be native to young people to actually want to revive the world they live in is only occasionally given serious thought. If it were, then the approach from the onset might be different. Instead of devising appealing ways to get students to swallow the planned diet set before them, the faculty might turn its most inventive attention to equipping students with the means of creating the world of new imagery, of imbuing those images with greater clarity and precision. But that would mean that the faculty would have to abandon what is the very core of its identity: the superior, esoteric knowledge by which it defines itself. What does this demand? It demands acknowledgement of the fact that there is a vast difference between conclusions already reached and distributed with pride, and the way of reaching conclusions. It would demand emphasizing in whatever the field of study and invention the differences between certainty of finished conclusions and conclusions-thus-far-reached. It would require intense focus on the relationships between the conceptual and the empirical worlds, between -- to put it bluntly -- the literal and the metaphoric. It would direct special attention to the limits of each, leading to a recognition of their fallacies.

But, of course, this would make education a dangerous undertaking, and college a place of even more than usual dreadful foment. In such an arena, the sacred is always being disturbed by challenge, and the keepers of the sacred constantly uneasy. If there are faculty who encourage such activities, they must surely be, to other faculty and to much administration, intellectual anarchists. Yet if there is any validity to the argument that we give to the unobservable the forms and features of what is observable by means of analogy, and that analogy is always by its very nature tentative, what other approach could we possibly make? So let us examine this more carefully.

Some Views of Metaphor

I have said that an analogy is but one type of metaphor. What is a metaphor then? *Webster's Unabridged Dictionary*, not always the best source in such terms, defines it thus: "The use of a word or phrase literally denoting one kind of an object or idea in place of another by way of suggesting a likeness or analogy between them." This seems to be clear enough, and quite understandable. More and more writings, however, take a thoroughly suspicious view of metaphor. Some call it mere ornamentation in writing; some, an effort to be glittery in expression; still others call it a matter of pretense, and not to be taken seriously, indeed to be avoided altogether. Metaphors only distract us from the serious, literal meanings. But you would take such a position only if you considered the world we live in to be made up exclusively of things which inevitably reveal their own inherent meanings. Ultimately, from this view, we become mere transcribers of that reality. Such a view has indeed been widely supported both in the arts and the sciences.

But others have pointed out that a metaphoric sentence is not simply an ornamental literal sentence, but a sentence performing an entirely different function and having an entirely different purpose than a literal statement. There has been a growing awareness that at the basis not only of literature but of science itself, there lies the metaphor which makes any science possible, and extending this, history, sociology, geology, anthropology, psychology, and other subjects of study.

Metaphors first appear as a play upon words, a pun, an absconding with a name and using it unexpectedly where it does not really belong. However familiar it may be, "jumping to a conclusion" is an absurdity because "jumping" belongs to physical, not mental, action. We tolerate this, however, because it is colorful and not really dangerous.

But what do we mean when we say a name belongs to a thing? Earlier, we had said that when we make a metaphor, we use a word that belongs to one thing but apply it to another. Well, in what sense do words belong to things? Although there are still a few who believe otherwise, most no longer believe that everything in nature has its name inscribed, in some way, within it. We cannot look at something and discover its name. So naming must be considered some kind of social agreement, an agreement which makes communication possible. All you need to do is remember how the name sounds, and understand that that set of letters has different meanings in different languages. *Gorge*, for instance, in English refers to a depression or a crevice in the land, but in French it refers to the throat or bosom. So when we say that words belong to events and things in ordinary perception, we must remember that we are talking about social conventions. Metaphors, then, will always be concerned with the ways in which we make transfers between conventional words or phrases. This would explain, in a fairly simple way, why a phrase that is readily recognized as a metaphor in one language, is treated as a literal statement when translated into another. Jokes in one language are not easily recognized as jokes in another.

This recognition of the linguistic limitations of metaphor and its sources in social convention leads to another suggestion which needs to be made. The means by which we come to control the things of the world we live in are all inventions. Some of these inventions are very old and some are as new as today's newspaper. The wisdom and the effectiveness of those who came before did not only provide us with mechanical inventions, but also with linguistic inventions for the expressed purpose of communication. New words are invented when older names and terms have been found insufficient for the handling of newer perceptions, new data, and newly developed concepts. We need new names when old ones no longer help to explain the explorations of things in the world.

There is even a more curious dimension to this. It appears when we come to look at the course of studies we are asked or obliged to follow in the pursuit of a degree. In whatever way it is organized, a curriculum almost invariably contains the accumulated knowledge of an age or of the ages. These are divided into segments, then pieced together in different ways, in response to the statistics distilled from previous records of previous students. Altogether, the subjects we study are supposedly accurate reflections of the world. All these pieces of "reality" are organized and divided into what are considered to be teachable segments. In whatever form these segments are cast, and by whatever tactics they are presented, the student is expected to listen. The students are expected to "grasp" what is being set before them, and if they also "gasp" it is a sign that they have learned something. Somehow, through the whole of these carefully modeled sequences, the material itself, beautifully and logically organized, will continue to hold its organization in the students' minds. The miraculous outcome is that the students learn to think without ever being aware that is what is being learned.

But when a student stumbles over a problem, a concept, a perception, the teacher comes forward, urging him to **THINK!** The upset student argues, "I am. I am trying to think." What should the teacher then say? "Make like a computer"? "Reflect upon the concepts in your mind"? "Look at the words before you"? All as useless and unilluminating as getting a child to walk by walking for him. At least, in that case, the child has a model to follow, even if he does not quite know that it is a model. For as I have argued, the specific act of thinking cannot be observed in the same way we can observe someone walking. So it remains a mystery that might or might not end in simple imitation of whatever external features present themselves, if any actually do. Yet there are just such features which can be suggested if we learn to use analogy.

This brings us back again to that primary question: what is thinking? It will not be a simple matter to explain. That means it will not take the form of a series of simple recipes to be followed in cookbook fashion. It will not follow a series of prescribed steps like some flow chart. And it will certainly be more complicated than what too often takes place in colleges; that is, listening to highly touted scholars expounding their conclusions on a variety of interesting, current problems. If you want to know just how complicated, notice that it will include explorations of meanings, concepts, communication, imagery, mimicry, ambiguity, reference, denotation and connotation. What has to be shown is that metaphor is the means by which new meanings and therefore new knowledge is created. It involves also the rejection (or at least suspension) of the belief that nothing new comes from the use of metaphor and that it is only a mode of dramatizing what is already known, or used for a time until the *real* nature of the event becomes increasingly apparent.

Functions of Metaphor

Metaphors do not function as simply alternatives to or as temporary substitutes for literal statements. They go far beyond the purpose of information transmission, which is the purpose of a literal statement. There are many important functions which metaphor performs that go well beyond information transmission. The most significant of these functions is the positing of enlarged contexts within which literal meanings are connected to implications not taken into account in the explicit literal meanings of a given statement. Here is a simple example: "The hat fits tightly" (literal); "The hat clutches my head" (metaphoric) suggests what the literal sentence does not.

A second function is the development of immediacy in the matter being discussed. There is, in our well-developed modern approach in the quest for meaning, the view that the history of an event, the historical origins of a theory, or of some thing, will explain that theory or that event. The trouble with this is that, as social psychologists have pointed out, any given theory or actuality is much more than what it was at its beginnings. That the branching of the tree contains more or less than what the seed contained at the beginning, and that knowing the origins does not necessarily make knowledge of the whole career possible. It may, to be sure, be a great interest to know origins, or roots, but such knowledge does not explain either the present state of a theory or of a fact. Put another way, theories or ideas have life histories. In a sense they are born, they thrive for awhile, and then they die. To know the origins of, say, relativistic physics at the start of the 20th Century does not necessarily lead us to understand how that theory is used now at the end of the century. Much has changed in Einstein's theory, as any theory must change over time. It is the metaphor that develops a context in the present world by employing what is familiar to what is unfamiliar or unknown at the moment. The form and the meaning of what we know become the form and the potential meaning of what we are seeking to know.

Let me offer a few more examples of this. There is undoubtedly value in understanding how Freud's psychoanalytical therapy allowed his patients to view their childhood as the source of adult maladies. What is more important -- at least for our work here -- is that Freud borrowed from classic Greek drama, for instance Sophocles' *Oedipus*, as a metaphor to explain a child's attitude toward the parent. There is value in knowing that Skinner extended the work of J.B. Watson. But it is far more enlightening to realize that the basis of Skinner's work is to be found in the mechanistic model of the engineer, of the mechanics of cause and effect through electrical behaviors of wires, filaments, and electrical flow, all of which are presently observable or measurable. In the act of comparing in order to use what we know to explain what we do not, to give meaning to what has no meaning as yet, both the unknown matter and the known will have to be observable in some way in the present.

Modern science has achieved some remarkable advances in its probing into the behaviors of matter and energy in the universe. Much of it has been accomplished by the invention of startling hypotheses, ones that fall within the scope of our thesis. Our conceptions of what the world contains derive from the theories with which we make our explorations and our experiments. What is startling about this is that it contradicts what has for centuries been our most basic common sense, namely, that the world and nature have traits and behaviors which are not determined by anything other than their innate forces and functions and structures, and that our observations of the world do not affect or alter that world. The alternate view that we have begun to discuss here seems to be saying that our thinking brings the world into existence -- that "thinking makes it so." Imagine for a moment the fantasy and fantastic worlds this would allow us to create! It would be like the wildest kind of science fiction we have ever read or have ever seen, since our imagination really knows no bounds. Imagine the monsters one could bring into existence just by thinking. Or the amazing animals and plants we could produce, merely by thinking. Of course, "thinking does not make it so." Everyone knows that!

And yet, psychologists and philosophers of certain schools, join with physicists in agreeing that to intrude upon nature and external events is to alter them in ways that nature alone could not. When we talk of matters which cannot be observed, we either say nothing, as Wittgenstein said, or we speak metaphorically, using what we can see and do know to describe what we do not see and do not know. By means of analogy then we create (make observable) what is not seen. So, in this sense, thinking does appear to "making something so." But I have already pointed out, this is profanity to those who believe that all knowledge preexists to our intrusions. People of this persuasion believe that knowledge only requires that we dig deeper, look closer, produce finer, more accurate instruments to discover finally *the* true nature of the event or thing. Metaphors, their thinking continues, have no place in any serious exploration into the nature of things. On the other hand, the presupposition of these realists and positivists are open to much debate. They reveal that concepts do determine what we "see" in nature, and what we can talk about. Their presuppositions have even decided in advance what we can and cannot talk about, or what we can and cannot think about. In their very arguments, they contradict their arguments.

If modern theories in science have shaken the idea of objective absolutes in truth and knowledge, the uncertainty which succeeds is nothing more than one of the basic principles on which quantum mechanics and relativity theories have been constructed. It appears to be suggesting that the so-called impenetrable chasm between science and poetry is not as impenetrable as an earlier thinking would have it. Perhaps what is being suggested as an alternative is that there is the possibility of proposing a concept of the unity of nature and of knowledge that previous concepts of science, poetry, and philosophy have not as yet permitted. Modern science does create what its practitioners can imagine.

What this does suggest is another, highly significant function of metaphor. The world we see owes its characteristics to the conception of the world contained *within* the metaphor we create and use. So metaphor becomes a conceptual instrument for the creation of a *reality-in-the-making*. To recognize this is to be advised, in a sense, of the responsibility of metaphor invention: don't be all that free and easy with your inventions, for they might become real in unanticipated, even undesirable ways.

Oddly enough, concepts which are metaphors can ultimately be tested in the active, empirical world. If this is a guard against over-imaginative projections, it is also a guard against falling prey to mysticism and ghoulish fantasies. The only trouble is that we rarely know in advance what is ghoulish and what is not; for ghoulishness is often a matter of social morality. Recall the trials of Dr. Frankenstein who adhered to the metaphor of "life as electricity" as he created his monster, much to his own dismay and to that of the townspeople.

In addition, metaphor makes possible an intimacy that nothing else can foster. This is, curiously, an odd but important function. Predicated on the idea that what we know best is what we are involved with directly and immediately, what we have "put our hands into," metaphor makes it possible to connect the unknown and sought-for with that which we have experienced directly already. This is what intimacy means in this case.

For the moment, a final, function which metaphor makes possible. Since the unknown is just that, unknown, and therefore featureless and without discernible functions and processes, the metaphor through transfer provides tentative recommendations in the form of hypotheses for both feature and function of that which is unknown.

Until we recognize this and the other functions identified, however, metaphor is little more than a literary device of doubtful merit. It is then seen as an ornament, which more often than not obscures rather than clarifies meaning. When there is an over-enthusiastic use of metaphor, the confusion becomes so deep as to reach into absurdity.

A metaphor does not just represent an actual event or an actual relationships between events. It may use such representations, but its purpose is to recommend how to think about events relative to one another, whose actual relationships are among the unobservable of what we take to be the real world. It is a proposal for giving meanings to events which, in isolation, have no inherent meaning at all. If you keep this in mind, you will see that the ornamental use of metaphor makes it all but impossible to consider what we call its epistemological function, namely, the ways in which we give meaning to events. It is by means of metaphor that we propose sometimes unexpected and out of the ordinary relationships, sometimes familiar, whose only uniqueness lies in the way those familiar things are connected. To follow the argument here is to give you an idea of how truly complicated the act of thinking is, no matter how incredibly fast it takes place or how easily it comes to some people.

Conditions for Metaphor Use

In developing and using metaphors several conditions will be present, one of which will work as the reason for doing so. Each calls for further illustration. Sometimes we find ourselves faced with a gap between observable matters. In order to get a complete picture, to see the whole event, the gaps must be filled with conceptual suggestions that would create a complete description. So we must posit a metaphor that will do just that. Sometimes we deliberately want to deviate from the ordinary meaning of a word in order to employ another, yet legitimate meaning of a word in order to add implications that the first meaning does not permit. Sometimes we borrow a word from some other area or discipline because that word carries with it the extended meaning which holds equally rich promise for the new context. Sometimes we find ourselves in a situation where there is no world available to us, so we are obliged either to invent one, or to borrow one and apply it where it ordinarily has never been used. And, sometimes we find it advisable to paraphrase an entire idea and put it into a heretofore unwarranted new context.

In each case, either we are seeking to develop new information within a familiar context or familiar material, or we are deliberately seeking to make more luminous and more emphatic for the purpose of focusing on aspects of ideas and meanings already contained within the original statement, but until then given little centrality. Metaphor is often used to focus attention on some particular aspects of an idea, to emphasize some aspects or features and to de-emphasize others, thereby underscoring what we deem important.

But if you examine these five conditions, it will be observed that they are all focused on the linguistic side of metaphor. That is, that the conditions of language alone, its strengths and its limitations, its vagaries and its ambiguities, our grasp of language or our ignorance of it, are all conditions for the constructions of metaphors. This would make it appear as if metaphor is the very special instrument for overcoming linguistic inadequacy. This is especially so when no word appears to exist that might be used. Now this would be reasonable enough argument, considering the fearful limitations which language imposes on us. We are always running beyond our skills in language and communication, always scrounging around for words, always on the verge of inventing new ones and expanding the dictionary, or borrowing words from other contexts and other disciplines, summoning them to work for our special purposes. But if this were the only reason for using or inventing metaphor, then we would have to admit that metaphor is really only a temporary tool for overcoming abysmal, but momentary ignorance. It assumes that if we expanded our vocabulary, we would never need to use metaphors. If this were the case, then all of the arguments against the ungainliness of metaphor use would be indeed valid.

But it must be evident that metaphor is much more than a matter of linguistic incompetencies. It is possible to create a series of conditions of the empirical world which we live in, and continue to grope into, which makes metaphor more than simply a matter of verbal inadequacy. Such a list would even prove to be the reasons, not the causes, for that linguistic inadequacy that always plagues us. These conditions are both empirical and conceptual, and when we confront them, we discover that far from showing metaphor to be the instrument of incompetence, it is in fact the most powerful means we have for creating new realities. For there is a difference between not knowing a language and there being no language as yet. Existing language is simply not relevant, as was the case at the turn of the 20th Century when the language of classical physics could not be used to describe quantum mechanics.

It should not be construed that language is unimportant or peripheral to our problem. Quite the contrary! What it means is that language is the only way we have of understanding the empirical world in any practical way. We must keep in mind also that language is a human invention, and that no language is adequate for all time, all things or all concepts. It is by means of linguistic symbols that we order the world, control it, reconstruct it, summon up the past, envision the future, produce images of what no longer exists, what does not yet exist, even of what could never exist. That is just the point. Language is much more than just a matter of words or of playing with words. It is the matters of sentences that carry meanings, connotations, information, intentions, expression of feelings which would go otherwise unexpressed. It is the instrument that we use to address the matters of the world that surrounds us, that we live in and by. It is, as philosophers have long argued, the universe of discourse of how we come to grips with the universe of experience. If we are to get a richer appreciation of the functioning of metaphor, we would do well to attend to what the metaphor does with the universe of experience.

We discover that by means of the metaphor we can use the ordinary things of the world in extraordinary ways. This groping for language is a good deal more than a manifestation of verbal ineptitude. More likely, it is a manifestation of trying to fit what we have available to us, our linguistic capacities, to the events we continue to encounter, and to invent new linguistic forms where none exist. It is the features, the functions, the relationships, the qualities of events in the world, that must be addressed. For it is to these that we apply the metaphors available to us or create new metaphors for doing so.

Conventions, Inventions and Metaphors

Perhaps the best way to approach this very complicated problem is to begin with the way the world comes to us. It is often argued that every facet of our lives, certainly at the outset, is shaped and directed by the conventions into which we are born. Now, you may have a little difficulty with this at first, because one of our more familiar conventions in the modern world is predicated on the notion that we are all born with a human nature or a "spirit" that transcends any environment. That is, that there are certain powers we possess at birth that determine our destinies, upon which no environment can impede. It can be summed up in the widely held view that if you are born with musical genius, for example, you will find your way to music in spite of anything that the environment can do to prevent it; that if you have a mathematical mind, not even a bad education will destroy that mind. Just as curious is the realization that sexual metaphors have been at the basis of certain distinctions made about science and scientists. As far back as Plato, as far forward as Francis Bacon, "mind" was seen as masculine, "nature" as feminine, and science as a lawful marriage between them both. Nature is to be dominated and controlled by masculine mind, which is why women were not generally scientists. When they were, it was evident that they were more masculine than feminine, no matter what other biological evidence was present. To be sure, it would be all but impossible to prove such claims without identifying first the conventional metaphors at work. It would even be hard to decide what kind of evidence would, in fact, prove or disprove it.   Certainly, simple anecdotes, such as the story of Mozart's development or Einstein's or Marie Curie's would hardly be sufficient without a careful examination of the intellectual and social climates in which each of them lived. And if we did this, we would then have to evaluate the impact and the limitations of those environments on their achievements.

If we now add another obvious fact -- that no set of conventions is so absolute or so fixed that they cannot be altered and that contradictions within them cannot arise -- you will begin to get a sense of yet another of the functions of metaphor. And if you are very sharp, you might even anticipate that it is by means of accepting alternate metaphors that conventions are challenged and finally rebelled against.

The concept of convention has already been introduced in Chapter One. We will have to expand on the definition offered previously. Conventions are the organized patterns of behavior and belief that direct us in our lives. They are the agreements that have been reached, formally or informally, of how to proceed in our day to day living. They go from the ways of speaking with one another, to methods of hunting and gathering, or earning a living or celebrating aspects of our lives, from marriage, divorce, raising children, organizing family life, political systems, structuring hierarchies in social relationships, playing games, holding disputes, writing and sustaining laws, on and on; covering the whole spectrum which comprises a given culture, a given society, a given civilization.

These conventions, which specify the rules by which our lives are conducted, become buffers against the chaos of worlds beyond a given culture or civilization. They give us our language for the purpose of communicating our very perceptions, even the intellectual foundations from which we reach out into the world around us. They prescribe the goals and rules of our behavior, as well as the rules for evaluating the behavior of others. They set the limits of what we tolerate and what we will not tolerate. They enshrine our moral codes and our conceptions of what the universe contains and what it does not contain.

In short, it has been said that they provide us with the whole of what is second nature to us: those beliefs and activities, expectations and limits that have become so much a part of our daily patterns of behavior and belief that we no longer question or challenge, and rarely have the courage to reject or to substitute, lest we be labelled heretic. For what our conventions do is reduce the sense of danger that might ordinarily prevail among men and women who are by nature, it is thought, dangerous. They make life predictable, and therefore peaceful -- if not always harmonious.

None of this should be very surprising to you. What might come as a surprise, however, is the notion that every one of these conventions derives from, or rests upon, some root metaphor which has long been accepted as a truth and is no longer open to challenge. But, of course, challenges do rise. If we think of conventions as formal and informal rules of relationships among people, individuals and groups, we might understand how it is that they become establishments. Such intractable adherence to the conventions of one group leads to the beliefs in the supremacy of one group over another, one race over another, one religion over another. To see this with clarity, just consider the structure of social conventions in South Africa and its laws of apartheid. The result of the rigid holding of such metaphors-turned-dogmas in a world where communication has become so uncontainable, is to intensify the commitment to find alternative metaphors when prevailing ones cause horror. The inevitable outcome is revolution, terrorism, devastation, murder. What began as linguistic formulations for purposes of providing an order in a random universe, resulted in sets of laws that govern further speech, behavior, and moral outlooks for societal living.

Metaphor is misused when further thinking is blocked: when the metaphor, upon becoming dogma, makes further thinking no longer necessary or possible. If you want to know how this looks consider the history of Germany from 1932 to 1945, the Soviet Union under Joseph Stalin, Italy from 1922 to 1945, America during the McCarthy years, or Saddam Hussein in the 1990's. In every case the metaphors of purity, supremacy, the "perfect society," the one "true religion" ended in passionate dedication to a given ideology, where thinking was no longer required, or more dangerously, even permitted. To do so would be to court getting yourself murdered, exiled or declared insane and then incarcerated.

Our metaphors are at the basis of the images we have of the "good life," and are the conventions we call upon to justify our behaviors and the things we believe and say. Against such dangers, we can understand the arguments against metaphor. They are dangerous as ideologies, we say, because they are prejudgments, categorizations of people and situations before we have even had a chance to explore them and to discover their actual characters. Except for one thing, at least. Even the notion of opposing prejudgment in this way is itself a prejudgment.

The functioning of such metaphor-based conventions is hardly limited to the political and religious areas. They go deeply into the core of our most ordinary activities. They determine the forms and the contents or our modes and qualities of our communications, the very clothes we wear, the way we wear them, the way we relate to others, the way we do business, the professions we enter, even our most intimate moments in our sexual relationships, our dedications as to what is moral and what is immoral. But we rarely, if ever, argue out our disagreements in the terms of the metaphors which gave them form. What we generally do is to claim that we are following the laws of nature itself, predicated, you will remember, on "masculine" science. Usually, however, what our conventions have determined "unnatural" fly in the face of all the evidence that nature itself makes available to us. So the metaphors themselves even provide us with the basis for our judgments of what is in tune with the laws of nature and what is not. Even the so-called "laws of thought" derive from some metaphoric basis. Mathematics, it has been argued, rests upon metaphor. Of course, the growing field of cognitive psychology and studies in the structure and function of the brain and its relation to our concepts of mind complicates the matter to a serious degree, and obliges us to look more carefully at the lines which distinguishes the universe of experience from the universe of discourse; that is, what we encounter in the primary world from what we say about it in the secondary worlds we invent.

There seems to be no way of getting around or avoiding the use of metaphor. If thinking is to take place, metaphor is both an empirical and epistemological necessity. The only thing left then is to examine the structure, the function and the types of metaphors available. This we will do in the next chapter. This must be done so that when they are used we can identify them and understand the rules of thinking which they impose. The fact that the misuse of metaphors produces models of relationships which are destructive of what we would be willing to call appropriate ways of living is not sufficient reason for abandoning the uses of metaphor altogether. Analysis shows this to be impossible. What it does oblige us to do is to measure the use of metaphor against the requirements of the continued act of thinking.

Common Sense and Everyday Thinking

Whatever grand contributions the college study of such select fields as psychology, art, history, physics or sociology provide for students in active pursuit of august careers, I suspect that the even more important role of thinking is to be found in non-professional, daily living. Is there a connection between the world of the everyday and the world of study and scholarship? Of course there is, although ordinarily we tend to separate the two; sometimes with good warrant, sometimes with a self-protecting act which seems to justify a feeling of inadequacy in the face of eggheads. But I think it is safe to say that if there was no connection, if the "world of gown" and the "world of town" were all that separate, there would be little except elitist reasons for going to college, including the usual reasons that are generally identified as getting a better job. For by obtaining a better job one gets into a better class of society, mingles with the decision makers of the world, becomes a decision maker him/herself and will be able to move into a better neighborhood with a bigger house. And perhaps this is reason enough for going to college and preparing oneself for membership in a profession.

But what surrounds us in our ordinary, day-to-day lives suggests something rather different. I think it reasonably safe to say that what the deep thinkers of the world of gown develop as knowledge and perception comes finally to shape the common sense of the world which is the town. Our ordinary conversation, little by little, is formed by the metaphors, the language, and the visions made available to us by those elitist eggheads, not only for students who do go to college, but for those who do not. Those who do not attend institutions of higher learning read newspapers and books, watch movies and television, attend dinner parties, raise children, play bridge and bingo, and are expected to participate in society. If what scholars do does not altogether influence people to alter and enrich their ways of thinking through problems, it assuredly gives them a language which is a different vision of reality than their ancestors, immediate or remote, had available to them. This will become evident your first visit home after starting college. Parents will revel in what you have learned, not so much about the volume of what you know, but how your speech, your ideas, your convictions will have changed since you left the August before.

For all of us, then, it is now common sense to look at a painting and analyze the psychological motivations of the painter, the psychological effects of the work, the psychological concepts that produce this or that effects on the viewers. The same thing happens at a play, and in later discussions. We comment on the psychological validity of the characters of the play, of the meanings of the play as a whole, or what it tells us about our own lives and the lives of others, how it explains or fails to explain the life of our own Uncle Otto.

Now, where did this approach and kind of criticism come from, except from the works of Freud and the efforts of professional psychologists to shows it relevance to our daily lives. Can we not say then that a test of Freud's greatness is the degree to which his very carefully developed metaphors and models of explanation have become part of the day-to-day perspectives of generations of people? Of course, the technical subtleties and precise distinctions made in his models get watered down and come to be accepted as literal statements about human behaviors and motivations. But this, for the most part, is less important than the fact that he has given us handy terms and ready classifications for understanding what might have been incomprehensible at an earlier period. Further, he has given playwrights, poets, and choreographers new visions to write or to choreograph their works. The world of the arts in simply drowned in psychological concepts, and we are never at a loss as to what to say about a play or a painting.

A century ago, comments on plays, novels, poetry, were not at all psychological. They were moral analyses, social observations, economic commentary. There had as yet been no Freud to give us modern perceptions. Perhaps the most interesting point in all this is the fact that we use such metaphors as are created for us and which give us a new vision with new classifications for talking about something we have always talked about in other terms, in other classifications. Give someone a clear, systematic way of looking at things, some will seize upon it with delight and gratitude, although perhaps unspoken. They probably will not question its scope, or validity, so long as they have a new vision. When this happens to a large number of people in a society or a culture, the level and quality of "common sense" is altered, and previous forms and levels are relegated to the realms of quaintness because "we don't think like that anymore." The point of all this is simply this: the metaphors we live by in any age are not the invention of simple minds, but of those whose imagination is remarkably inventive, whose attention to detail in a world becoming increasingly complex, in increasingly deepening perceptions. If we misuse them, fail to appreciate their status as metaphors, are unaware of the alterations they make in our understanding and in our powers of thinking, it is nevertheless these "uncommon" people who have enriched our common sense.

There are common sense ways of bringing up children, of eating, or exercising, of seeing a play, or warming a home, of driving a car, of loving the Lord, of reading a book, of performing an experiment, of learning a language, or of loving your country. And these common sense ways do not derive from a long reservoir of tradition moving forward in time, but from the creative acts of developed thinking working backwards toward those who have not themselves developed those skills, but now can live on the dividends of that creativity. The very hierarchy of modern valuing reflects not the past, but the newer metaphors made available to us in the vastness of modern media. If there is a clash in values, it is rarely apparent in the behavior of the younger members of a generation. It is invariably found in the concerns of the elders for whom the new metaphors are disturbances or threats against older metaphors, older value hierarchies. Acquaint yourself with some of the new theologies being written within the very bosom of the old -- the writings of Hans Kung, Edward Schillebeeck and Karl Barth. Consider the anger manifest among supporters of more traditional metaphors, and you will see this impact in modern religion. The perception of Divinity changes with shocking impact on common sense until that common sense dissolves into new forms, and becomes commonly shared by any group of the faithful.

It is this way too that alters the forms of arguments between "town and gown," between work and school. The ideas that once guided our concepts of work, success, advancement, no longer have much influence. We no longer think in terms of beginning at the bottom and, through time and diligent apprenticeship, work our way to the top. We now go to the Harvard Business School, receive training and a degree, and begin at middle management. (Do you prefer Columbia, Cornell or Ohio State? No matter. The model is quite the same.)

The world we see is the world constructed from the metaphors that serve as their bases. It is for most of us, the only world we see. Any other world, beyond the accepted ways, is either very alien or needs to be reorganized into the accepted conventions. And it is this that becomes the form of our current common sense approach to the problems of everyday living. At any rate, that common sense is not native or inborn. It is not a prearranged response to the world in the terms of that world. It is learned in the most casual, informal, unconscious way, and it determines our behaviors and our perceptions. It is therefore, neither illogical not mysterious. One could trace the changes, growth, declines, regeneration of a culture by the analysis of the changes in common sense. And whatever changes do occur derives from the thinking by those uncommon men and women who have developed new perceptions of the world around us and how we are to think about it.

Summary

I have argued that metaphor involves a transference of one thing seen as another. In this chapter I have also discussed several functions of metaphor during the thinking act. I have argued, I hope effectively, against what is called the realist view that states that our world is there only to discover rather than invent. Moreover, the creation of new metaphors creates a society's common sense of viewing the ordinary, day to day events. Accepting this requires in our own thinking a new attitude regarding knowledge and the conventions of our existence. In accepting this thesis, one easily realizes that thinking is no more a mystery than any other skill to be taught and learned.

Now, if you consider any skill that you have learned already, you probably realize that it is composed of other smaller skills that, when done in unison, show competence in the larger skill. For example, driving a car involves steering, road judgment, gear shifting, speed maintenance and so on. When one has mastered each of these individually and collectively, we can say that the person can drive. In a very similar way, to say one can think effectively, we must be aware that in that activity there are several associative skills that must first be mastered before we can claim to be competent in effective thinking. So we need to explore the various types of metaphors to show the particular features of each, under what circumstances each is used, and finally substantiate my claim that the use of metaphor is essential to the thinking act that forms the concepts, theories and sorting systems of the various disciplines.

4.

METAPHORS: TYPES AND

INTERNAL STRUCTURES

Having described in general terms the sequences that are followed when we engage in metaphor using, we have only prepared for the next phase of our exploration. If we are to become increasingly skillful and precise in the act of thinking, we must examine the particulars of the structures of the various types of metaphors. It is very much like looking at a work of architecture. We get one sense, one impression or understanding of it when we look at it from the outside, as a singular whole, and quite another, however complementary, when we explore it from within, identifying the various elements and how they are formed together to create that whole. From the side, we come better to understand how the whole is held together and makes possible the functions which the entire structure performs and permits. In much the same way, we must examine the inner structures of metaphors in all their various structures. Externally, metaphors are unities that make possible a number of generalizing cognitive functions. But when we examine their particulars, we recognize that there are some surprising distinctions which can be made in that thinking act which a metaphor generates, and some surprising differences to be discovered in the sorts of thinking that the types of metaphors make possible.

Recall the college campuses you have visited. While not all fit the following description, colleges do have old models that they try to live up to. These are models of august appearance, hinting at ivy covered walls, even when there is no ivy to be discovered. Nevertheless, when students first come to college, it is to a building or to a campus of buildings, that they come. The very appearance is expected to sober them to the idea that they are entering a domain in which the quest for *truth*, a search for what nature and humanity has to tell us about itself or themselves, is primary. I suppose that this first impact never altogether leaves us, though over time it is diminished by the more immediate impact of classroom activities and the teachers and their ideas that fill our days and our years. So we learn that it is not for the buildings, the external architecture, that we come to college, but the intellectual quests that go on inside those buildings, but which the buildings bespeak.

So with our work here. It is not simply with the general fact of metaphor that we are concerned, but with the specifics of thinking that particular metaphors sustain and direct. The externals of buildings and the end products of thinking may very well inspire us with awe and a kind of romantic reverence, with the eagerness to bow to experts and to appearances, to what surrounds us, and to those who are endowing us with their awesome wisdom. But when we become aware of the inner activities of both buildings and metaphor structures, perhaps we can discover or recover some of the sense of fun about the world -- that fun we had when we were much younger and thought the world was there for our making, like some fascinating toy to play with. We might discover again that the natural scientist, the artist, the historian, the social scientist does just what we did when we were children, but does it better, with freer, more sustained mischievousness and imagination arising from an awareness of possibilities which are beyond children. They may do it with an appearance of seriousness, in labs coats and smocks, with sophisticated cyclotrons and impressive sculptures, but play it is, nevertheless. Instead of blocks or small cars or dolls, the play is primarily with ideas that become the templates for reorganizing what we know and making their contribution to "how the world goes." This happens in historical analysis, in psychological investigation, in the probings into scientific data, in anthropology, sociology, continuously in philosophical thinking, and every other field of study you will embark upon in your college career.

Nevertheless, it must be remembered that the premise on which this book is based is itself an argument, and therefore, a source for disagreement. If you begin with the assumption that the only things we can really talk about are those things in the world that we can actually see, or will sooner or later see, and that everything else is a form of deception, self-deception, or mere talk, then metaphor itself, in whatever form, is mere pretense awaiting to be replaced by some irreducible, irrefutable truths. So the whole concept of metaphor, when taken seriously enough to permit playing with the world, requires us to alter our sternest and stodgiest views of what the universe is made of and what it is we can play with.

Remember how we defined metaphor. It is the transfer of concepts from areas they habitually occupy into areas that are strange, unfamiliar, unknown. It is seeing something we do not understand as something else that we do. We apply, to yet unknown aspects of the world, those concepts, words, images which have come to belong to what is ordinary to us. But the reasons for metaphor-making can create havoc with the world grown fixed and totally predictable. To discover the details of what constitutes metaphor, and how a metaphor is constructed, could provide great opportunity for irreverent fun, for delightful nose-tweaking of sacred cows, and enjoying the absurdities of some very odd inventions and some very old conventions. We might fear, or at least suspect, that certain external conditions of nature will impose limitations on what we can transfer to what. This is a notion that we need to discard immediately, because any transfer of the material to the immaterial, ascribing powers to the inert, seeing particulars as wholes are only limited by our imagination. This does not mean, however, that any transference is as good as any other. As we will see as this work unfolds, accepting one transference over another, one metaphor instead of another, will be related to criteria for acceptance in each of the disciplines. It is by this time generally agreed that no matter how long you may stare at the world or at a given event, that world or event will tell you nothing except what a concept, derived from some metaphor, illuminates for you. It is for this reason that the more that you understand the structure and the function of the types of metaphor in use, the more you will be able to recognize what some segment of the world is contained in its language and by contrast what its limitations are. So thinking begins and ends in some metaphor which is a screening of the external world. Inevitably, it deepens with the analysis of that metaphor, with an alteration, substitution or discovery of a richer clarification. Moreover, understanding now comes to mean a comprehending of what is contained in the metaphor, and how and what the metaphor makes present in the world defined, described and explained in a particular metaphor.

Species of Metaphor

So let us examine the various types of metaphor that have been identified, how they are formed, what thinking they make possible, and what limits they put on our thinking. I will list seven of these, and then identify their distinctiveness, remembering that every type of metaphor is a transfer from what is familiar to what is not, in order to make the unknown comprehensible within the terms of the known. The seven I will consider are *ANALOGY, SYNECDOCHE, METONYMY, CATECHRESIS, IRONY, PATHETIC FALLACY* and *OXYMORON*. These should suffice to give a clearer picture of particular metaphors, and their function and limitations in the thinking act.

ANALOGY

This much can be said for analogies: we never have trouble inventing them. We seem to find ourselves almost compelled to do so whenever we have difficulty explaining or describing some matter to someone more confused than we. The only time we have trouble is when an analogy does not clarify an explanation. Also interesting is the fact that we never seem to have any difficulty in finding weaknesses in other people's analogies. This is because, whether we know it or not, we are working with a contrary analogy of our own, and refuse to accept someone else's. When conflict arises in such cases, the dilemma is likely twofold. First, there is the psychological problem of overcoming the resistance of those who love their own analogies or because they rely totally on them for their own understanding and unwilling to accept the analogies of others. The second and more interesting difficulty lies in the demand on us to show the basis in similarity of relevance between the analogy suggested and the matter being discussed. These are reasons enough (at least for now) to justify the need to analyze the elements that comprise analogies.

I have earlier talked about the requirement of courage imposed on students. Nowhere is this more pertinent as in the examination of analogies. For here, in the development of other modes of perception which analogy offers, we come upon the fears of a loss of identity, of self, of commitments earlier held, as analogy might impose upon us. If, for example, I can no longer believe that the world is structured in a harmony that makes human life possible, what can I believe? What will protect me from awful chaos in the world that is simply indifferent to me?

I will tell you, although timidly at this point: find a better analogy than the musical analogy of harmonics. You can't tell what new and interesting possibilities may open for you.

In its strictest sense, an analogy is composed of four terms, though they are not always made explicit. When we analogize, we are saying that the way in which any first two terms (say, A and B) are related is also the way in which the last two terms (say, C and D) are related. The important term here is "relates." When the terms are spread out, they look like this: "A relates to B as C relates to D." A horse is to its jockey as a ballplayer is to his coach. Or, as a train is to its engineer. Or, as a computer is to its programmer. Now, if you are going to look for *truth* in an analogy, it will be easy to find it, but easier still to find "*untruth*" in it. All you must do is to point out even the smallest difference in the relationship between the second two (C and D) as compared to the first two (A and B). For instance, coaches do not ride their ballplayers as a jockey rides his horse. But if you are intent on doing that, you will be missing something far richer, far more meaningful. Analogy is built upon resemblance between otherwise seemingly different events, one of which is very familiar; the other of which we are seeking to explain. But a problem arises when there is the expectation that the resemblance should be readily apparent. This turns out to be a problem of misexpectation, since more often than not, a recommended analogy has the purpose to suggest that one should "see" the familiar in what is for the moment unfamiliar. So when someone says, "Oh, that's a bad analogy," what might be implied is that no resemblance or similarity is evident in the relationships between the two things being discussed. But often it is precisely because there is little or no apparent similarity that gives justification and luminosity to the analogy being offered.

Analogy is probably the most widely recognized and frequently used type of metaphor because it does not specifically or explicitly indicate what is being transferred: it is only implied. The kinds of relationships that can be transferred include a quality, a feature, or even a function. What it is ascribing can only be discovered in the context of the discussion and the observations that follow. Some trivial examples: upon seeing someone working strenuously with heavy burdens, someone might say, "the man is a pack-horse." Or, while referring to someone who resists altering his ways of behaving or thinking, we might claim that, "he's a mule." Describing a unique quality, we might say, "she lights up the room with her smile." The first suggests a resemblance in functional relationships; the second, of the relationships of features; and the third, those between qualities. And indeed, we can with a little imagination see resemblances between the most disparate matters, and still be effective in its use. However, as I have said, these are trivial, for they add little beyond what we can observe directly and immediately. Thus they offer nothing new or surprising. But when someone suggests an analogy between, say, the Soviet Union's conduct in Afghanistan and our country's role in Vietnam, the very memory of our country's experience in the latter is saying a great deal more than simply describing some ordinary behavior in an uninspiring, ordinary situation. The reference now is to a set of relationships which describe a whole history of tragedies, incompetencies, what some have called cruel and needless deaths, deceptions, unmitigated horrors.

The dramatic character of analogy becomes even clearer when we encounter the recommendation that the internal structure and behavior of the atom is best seen as resembling a solar system. Here we have a situation in which we identify what cannot ever be seen with something which can be seen. (Interestingly, we have never been able to "stand back" from our solar system and "see" its structure!) In a similar way, light is seen alternately as waves (derived from a water analogy) and photons (particles or packets of energy) or Darwin's natural selection is derived from animal husbandry (artificial selection).

One final point here which leads into the next type of metaphor to be discussed. When an analogy leads to a more critical examination of the detailed elements contained in what is being analogized, we discover that what we thought was simply an analogy was, in actuality, an example of synecdoche. Let us turn to this, though we will come back to analogy several times.

SYNECDOCHE

In synecdoche what we do is connect a number of features in such a way that they are envisioned as one major feature. Again, some trivial examples, to show what this means, and then some serious ones. We have always identified actors and actresses by some single feature which is so marked that the one feature will identify the whole person. So, an actress is called "The Body," an actor is called "Schnozzola" (The Nose), a third is called "The Face." Now, no one really believes that the person so identified is nothing more than this one feature. Yet the others are de-emphasized by being noted as being too ordinary or unimportant to be noted or paid attention to.

What it is important to notice is that where analogy does not refer at all to specific features, but rather emphasizes relationships among things, synecdoche always refers to a thing, an external object or a specific observable feature. Perhaps a more amusing illustration of synecdoche is to be found in caricature, those drawings done by political and theatrical cartoonists. You recognize that in the cartoon a specific feature or two are so exaggerated that the whole drawing has become a comment on some feature of the subject of the drawing, a comment in which the whole of the character of the subject appears to be summed up in the exaggeration.

But, of course, the most interesting aspect of the uses of synecdoche comes to us in truly unexpected places and analyses. And because they are not always recognized as such, the synecdoche is mistakenly read as a literal report of the whole idea or character or some particular event. This happens in historical studies, in psychological studies, perhaps especially in the physical studies of the surrounding universe. A military history of a country, for example, in which every other aspect of that nation's existence is to be understood as a consequence of its military career, is synecdoche. A psychological thesis in which the whole of a person's existence is determined by one force, whether it be "sex," "power," "spirit" or otherwise, is synecdoche. And there is always the suspicion that the physicist who has been persuaded that the ultimate building blocks of the universe have been found might be engaging in the use of synecdoche. In all these case, a physical, psychological, or metaphysical complexity is characterized by the nature, function and career of a single observable feature.

METONYMY

This is unquestionably the most difficult type of metaphor that we can use, and because of that, the most easily overlooked as a form of metaphor. First of all, it shares with synecdoche the use of a part of a feature to represent the whole of that event. But it does so by reversing the synecdochal tactic. It sees a whole when only a part is actually involved. So, for example, the White House is said to have made a decision when in fact it is the President who had done so. We sometimes say that "man will not tolerate certain kinds of behavior" when we really mean that this man or this group is opposed to it. We sometimes read "the Church holds that ..." when, in fact, it is a pope, a bishop or one group that "holds that." I think you can see how metonymy, when used improperly, can lead to misinterpretation by many; that what is said by one person or one select group actually came for the entire population.

But be sure you do not misconstrue the analysis here. It can all too easily be read as condemnations of the errors that metonymy produces. The most that can be said, you will understand that misuse produces mischief. Its proper use, like the judicious use of wine, produces surprisingly stimulating thought.

The most interesting form of metonymy is the deliberate or unguarded shifting of cause and effect, or effect for cause. We often, for example, hear someone say that "the symptom is being treated," as if it were the cause, when actually it was an effect. To say this is to point out that unwittingly someone has been constructing metonymy without knowing it, and is, therefore, either misleading oneself or others. But the much more interesting point to consider is what is actually involved in this business of transferring cause and effect. When we speak of causes we are invariably attempting to determine what event was to be ascribed as having produced the effect of outcome that we now observe. This means that we are seeking some observable thing or event that we can point to, and state that this produced or caused that. But causes, we discover, are not things. Rather, they are concepts we employ to account for what cannot be seen, the actual connection of events that produce a sequence.

Some have identified causes as purely psychological efforts to be inserted between events so that continuity is established. Others have rejected the notion of this psychological perspective, and have argued that the principle of cause and effect is a logical instrument for reading out implications between disconnected events. And what finally is accepted as providing us with a reasoned connection between an event we can observe (the effect), and some unobservable act that cannot be observed. So, we argue about the cause of war, of disease, of growth, of decline, of the death of a culture, of a state of happiness, or of the achieve-ment of success, of failure, and the like. Now, because such causes are, in principle unobservable, there is no way of fixing, with any assurance, what is cause and what is effect. Thus, the transfer of cause and effect actually means that by metonymy we are simply providing an alternative to accommodate the accepted views of viewing matters. If it were not this, then every metonymy would simply be either a mistake in observation or a deplorable judgment whose purpose it is to confuse the honest among us. But since it is a suggestion for alternate ways of envisioning or imagining the range of possibilities which nature itself might permit, metonymy is the metaphor of fruitful alternatives.

This matter of cause and effect becomes pivotal in the uses of metaphor, especially in metonymy. For, contrary to what we have learned, the distinguish-ing between them is far from simple, thus there is good reason for difficulty. Causes, after all, are concepts which we invoke or construct or ascribe to an event. You cannot see cause. You can only infer it. All you see is one event and then another event. If you need to make a connection, you must do so symbolically that serves as the connecting link. And when you go about providing it, all you can do is to present some logical linguistic evidence, usually in the form of a deductive demonstration that, all alternative concepts considered, it is reasonable to conclude that *this causes that.*

Another example of this to illustrate the conceptual nature of causes. Consider two billiard balls on a pooltable. You strike one which rolls and strikes another. You will conclude that the first ball hitting the second *caused* the effect of the ball rolling away. Sounds simple enough, doesn't it? But look again, this time more closely. Upon closer examination, we find no inherent quality of the first ball that will cause it to move the second. Its color, weight, shape, shininess, and the like will not change as a result of hitting the second ball. We can infer correctly that if some inherent quality of the first ball was not responsible then something else must be. Our training in junior high science classes will tell us that the first ball exerted a force on the second which resulted in its rolling away. Now notice the shift here: no longer is the ball the cause, but the force of the ball. The skeptics among us might ask, "show me the force." Obviously you cannot directly observe forces; they do not have substance, volume or weight. *Force* is a concept that is inferred backwards to exist to explain the result or effect of that cause. If this begins to sound rather complicated, let me suggest that it can even be more so when we ask, "What caused the first ball to have a force to begin with?" or "How do I know that rolling is the direct effect?" Here, now, you must rely on another series of conceptual devices to introduce another concept called "kinetic energy."

Now, logical proof is not empirical evidence or actual, observable proof. Some have called concepts of cause strictly psychological, meaning a projection onto external events. Others have emphasized its logical structure. But in either case, the modern world has, by and large, come to acknowledge that we do not see *causes*.

In some way, and for purposes of producing pictures for consistency in the world, we ascribe causes, since this is a way of connecting otherwise disconnected events. All this leaves the whole affair quite up in the air. It is bad enough when it appears that we have all of the materials actually before us here and now, and all we have to do is invent a link. But think how really difficult it is when what we are considering are events that happened years ago, in distant places, where we have nothing but records of the past to stare at. Here all we begin with is the optimism that what those records tell us is what actually, without any doubt, really took place. So we (meaning we who are groping about for persuasive connections) develop arguments and proposals for what is a cause and what is an effect. We argue about what is the cause of a culture's growth or decline; about economic developments or failures; about human behaviors; all those matters that require from us some explanation for its career. And in every case, what we have come to agree upon as the cause is just that: an agreement. And because it is an agreement, we come to recognize the role of metonymy -- that in areas where we cannot actually observe events, we are altering the sequential relationships which have been agreed upon, which we have taken to be the ordinary way of viewing those relationships. If it were not this, then every metonymy would be either probably wrong by actual, observable evidence, or it would be deviltry produced by some whimsical mind trying to amuse or to deceive us. But metonymy is not a tactic of confusion, deception or trickery. It turns out to be a suggestion for other ways of envisioning or imagining what cannot be observed in order to account for that which can be. Metonymy, then, is an affair of transferring accepted, agreed upon conceptual relationships, and thus, suggestions for the development of new ways of envisioning the relationships among things in the world we are dealing with.

We now move to catechresis, though, as with analogy, we will be returning to metonymy, as the analysis continues.

CATECHRESIS

It has been well argued that anything which we can see or any idea that we can think of can become the substance of a metaphor for whatever it is we are trying to explain or to explore. This, of course, does not mean that any thing will serve as well as any other thing in metaphor construction. But it does mean that the sources for metaphor and therefore for thinking are as unlimited as the world itself. With this great breadth of possibility open to us, it would be interesting to make some distinctions between possible reasons for the need for metaphors. There are probably more to be identified, but the following are a good beginning.

We sometimes come upon an event whose character we do not even know, either animate or inanimate; or have only a vague knowledge of some event whose intrinsic character we do not know at all. In order to explore, understand or explain what is not yet known we have either to invent a name for it, or borrow the name of something whose character we are not quite sure of. This happens, as I will show, quite often in psychology, very often in the physical sciences, and often enough in every other field. This invention is called catechresis, and it is a widely used type of metaphor. If metonymy is evidence of how little certainty there is about the knowledge of our world, catechresis is evidence of how often we encounter complete novelty in the world. Moreover, if a discipline, a field of study, can be defined as an activity of creating new models from which new knowledge is constructed, it is the metaphor of catechresis that is the instrument by means it all begins.

Catechresis is also the best type we have for discovering how, by means of metaphor, we transfer qualities into contexts which are not yet known, and thereby constructing new understandings. Illustrations of this are not hard to come by, though they may sometimes be difficult to grasp fully. The odd thing about catechresis is that once we have borrowed or invented a name, and that title has become accepted and familiar, its catechretic qualities dissipate. The metaphor takes on the qualities of the reality that has been borrowed. This makes it very much like the study of the unconscious which, being metaphorized into something that we are conscious of, ceases to be unconscious. Take an abstract term such as "education," the definition of which has been argued from the very early years right down to yesterday's newspaper. Education embraces so vast, and to the minds of many, so unlimited a field, that it resists being identified in any fixed way. So it remains a field of activities to which any number of names, characteristics and functions are attached. The result is that arguments about education, in effect, turn out to be arguments about its definition and what is to be included in those definitions. Writers in the field of education seem to have no choice but to borrow from psychology, from drama, from science, from mechanics, from religion, and, Lord knows, from what other fields, to describe and explain the nature and the purposes of education. Depending on what you call it, you state its purpose: development of character, teaching the "whole person," creating the gentleman or lady, nurturing the mind, gaining power through knowledge, fostering human qualities in barbarians, creating citizens, making communication among people possible, socialization, earning a living.... Can you think of any others? At one time each of these has been claimed as education's primary function and, thus, purpose. The role of catechresis here should be evident. As each new definition of education is proposed, a whole new set of recommendations, prescribed by the metaphor, are offered proponents gathered, test scores published, new research conducted, followed by new recommendations.

Is catechresis apparent in the field of the natural sciences? One might expect, however, that here at least, in dealings with things, operations and traits which depend upon observations, catechresis would never be appropriate. Yet in no other field is there so much inventing of new terms and new functions, or borrowing from neighboring disciplines. Indeed, it is hard to discover what term in physics has not begun as catechresis. Charm, spin, neutrino, quark, neuron, protons, X-rays, alpha-rays, beta-rays, black holes; until we begin to doubt that science has any term at all which is indigenous to itself, that has not been borrowed either from a broader common-sense vocabulary, or from some other, earlier discipline.

What is the point of all of this? Simply that since every discipline is a symbol-using, symbol-inventing activity, and since those symbols contain the meanings and the descriptions of the activities and the intentions of the field, the very borrowing illuminates the quest for understanding. To know what the words and the concepts refer to is to know the goal. And what catechresis does, as any metaphor does, is to direct attention to what is part of the fund of ordinary knowledge, captured in ordinary talk, and to transfer this to the matters before us, which is the object of our quest for knowledge and understanding.

But there is a special warning note that might be introduced at this point, for it occurs with particular force in this type of metaphor. Every metaphor, when it is used often enough, and becomes part of our usual thinking, appears to become transformed into a literal, descriptive statement. In analogy and synecdoche, it is fairly easy to discover this transformation, and to be on guard against misuse. It is not as easy in dealing with metonymy because the suggested relationship being talked about can make sense whatever the direction we give it. In catechresis, however, frequent use makes the transformation to reality not only a simple step, but a seemingly quite natural one. For once having borrowed a word or a concept from anywhere, and made it serve a new purpose where none existed before, its very use becomes accepted as a component means of communicating difficult (or simple) notions. So catechresis transforms easily into reality, and its metaphoric origins quickly, often permanently, are forgotten.

Now what this does, perhaps unexpectedly, is that it underscores something about the nature of "reality," something that we have already mentioned. If so much of reality turns out to begin as catechretic statements, then much of "reality" turns out to be pure invention on the part of imaginative men and women -- an idea which can do nothing but distress all the realists everywhere. Examples of this are not difficult to find. We have only to examine the fall of ex-President Richard Nixon to see this. Since 1974, there have been numerous reasons offered for the whole Watergate debacle. Some have argued that there existed purely political motives for the break-in and subsequent cover-up. Others have proposed that Nixon's own psychological make-up inevitably would lead to his demise. Still others have looked for evidence of moral explanation. Now, which of these is the *real* explanation? Obviously, none are: they are only interpretations with each based on different metaphors.

But just consider how many thought problems might be resolved if we take this seriously. The disputes over the nature of reality -- arguments about what is really real -- about why things might be real to you but not to me -- all might now be understood as rejections or acceptances of some basic catechresis. It is this very development in the physical sciences that has created what classical physicists and philosophers call the "mess in physics today." It is a mess because the old language of Newtonian physics is useless in the face of the new findings of modern physics. Now, neither Bohr, Einstein, nor Heisenberg approached the problem in these terms, but each camp came up with the same realization: in modern physics, the uncertainty in discovering firm knowledge, the whole concept of reality would have to be re-made, re-thought, re-defined. And Schroedinger is said to have moaned that he wished that he had never been involved in the discovery of quantum (a fine catechretic term which physics has made part of its and our ordinary vocabulary), because it would oblige him to re-define the concept of reality and abandon its standard, classical view.

Whatever the new definition of reality turns out to be, the basis of that definition seems to remain the same. What will be described and explained will be the tangible events we have, can or will experience. But what has been agreed upon thus far is that whatever enters into that experience, the instruments and the language in which it is made available, is a part of that experience. Thus, what is compromised is the absoluteness of the external world. Indeed, we must acknowledge that the world comes to us in some verbal, symbolic form. It is this that gives shape to and alters the external world from whatever it might have been before any observations were made. Moreover, we have finally agreed that on this basis there may not even be an external world until it has been intruded upon by us. An intrusion that is accomplished with our instruments, mechanical and linguistic, that the whole experience is couched in. A terrible thought for many! So metaphor, in some form, is as fundamental a part of reality as are the external objects we seek to explain. Try to think of a science without a symbol system. Would it even be possible? Try to think of science without a vocabulary especially invented (like the "quantum" already mentioned) or borrowed from ordinary language (like "force" or "natural selection") and given special meaning. Would that be possible? To the second question, the answer is a little uncertain, for ordinary language might be invoked to serve the needs of the investigator. But even there, confusion between reality and fantasy can only be avoided when its basis as metaphor is recognized and properly identified. So catechresis is a good deal more than pretense or trickery in science. At its very core, catechresis is both a manifestation of imagination and the instrument by which we can give form, function, and meaning to the external world.

IRONY

The dictionary defines irony as a form of dissimulation; saying one thing but meaning something different. We might even say that it is a matter of speaking metaphorically, but intending that the reader or hearer will take the statement literally. In a fuller context, another definition speaks of a state of affairs as ironic when it leads to the very opposite of what one would ordinarily expect. It is ironic, for instance, when in an effort to provide security for someone, the very effort puts him into greater danger than ever.

The second of these definitions makes it a little more difficult to see the broader metaphoric role which irony plays. In fact, why is irony metaphoric? The answer is that irony shows an aspect of metaphor we have not yet met.

Our natural tendency, as I have said earlier, is to read or to hear any statement for its literal meaning. The result is that we are sometimes distressed to discover that it was intended as irony. Here is a very funny example of irony. First, it is read or heard literally. Then, when discovered, it provokes anger in a victimized student. It comes from Joseph Heller's novel, *Good As Gold*,[1] and

---

[1]

Used with permission of Simon and Schuster.

shows irony at a couple of levels. Professor Gold is talking with one of his students, who is complaining about a course that Gold is giving:

> "Professor Gold,... I hope you won't mind if I tell you that I'm disappointed in the course."
>
> Gold sighed sympathetically. "So am I. What's *your* complaint?"
>
> "It's called 'Monarchy and Monotheism in Literature, From the Medieval to the Modern'..., but it seems to be a course in Shakespeare's history plays," said Epstein.
>
> "We'll be moving on to the major tragedies soon," Gold replies breezily. "All but *Othello* and the Roman plays. In *Othello*, unfortunately, there is no monarch, and the Romans were not monotheistic."
>
> "The course description in the college catalogue isn't accurate," Epstein complained.
>
> "I know," said Gold. "I wrote it."
>
> "Was that fair?"
>
> "No, but it was intelligent. We feel that anyone interested in literature ought to study Shakespeare and we know that few students will do so unless we call it something else."
>
> "But I'm not interested in literature. I'm interested in God. I became an English major because the English Department seems to be offering so many courses in theology and religious visionary experiences.... Should I switch to the Department of Religion?"
>
> "No, don't go there. You'll be reading Milton and Homer. Try Psychology if you're interested in God. I believe they've latched on to religion now."
>
> "Where are the psychology courses?"
>
> "In Anthropology. Soon everything is going to be in Urban Studies anyway, so you might as well major in that. But do it

soon. Otherwise, you might find me there in a year or two and have to read Shakespeare's history plays all over again."

A number of things are to be said here. The commentary of a cynical and frustrated professor are pretty funny. (He desperately wants to be Secretary of State.) Of course, his views and tactics are enough to make sober professors furious. But is there any danger that this might be read literally, as an accurate description of what might be going on in some college? Not much of a chance, since students could readily check this out, either directly or indirectly with other students who might have taken some of the same courses. And yet, students might not know the inner workings of various departments and the directions in which they are moving. But what it does show is what I mentioned at the beginning of Chapter Two: the insanity that appears to be a natural function in the internal workings of a college among students, faculty, and administration. So the irony becomes readily apparent in the comparing of these comments with what actually goes on, or should be going on, at any college.

What, then, is the metaphoric function of irony in this case? Here, especially, irony illuminates the psychological distance between sober intentions and the way things actually develop. The absurdity, when it is recognized, as it appears in this gap, lessens the tendencies toward the dogged pursuit of purity and absolute accuracy where those absolutes are unattainable. But then, this may be nothing more than bitterness presented in the form of satire, a matter of derisive exposition of human frailty, or stupidity, or pretentiousness, and does nothing more than appear as the expression of dissatisfaction of an individual who just despises himself and those around him. In that case, it would simple be a game, a verbal display of clever denunciation. All this is quite possible, were it not for the odd clue to a personal truth that is contained in the ironic series, the way in which an idea is developed over a series of verbal exchanges.

As with any metaphor, there is an implicit comparison here which serves as the foundation on which any metaphor is built. What would have been a literal statement covering the same ideas? It would require direct reports of which department is teaching which courses, without necessarily taking other courses into account. Such a report would, if requiring justification, call upon another literal statement drawn from within the content of the courses themselves. What the metaphor does is to enlarge the context within which a specific course is being considered. Moreover, along with this enlarged context for comparison purposes, there is also intruded, sometimes bluntly, sometimes subtly, a value commentary on the perceived relationship among various efforts, in this case,

courses and the departments that offer them. If Professor Gold's comments are
too blunt, they take on the character of personal vindictiveness, and can easily be
dismissed by readers and hearers. If subtle, there is a chance that whatever
personal pique is present will be transcended by the form of the exposition whose
purpose, after all, is to illuminate a situation, a complete concept, and its qualities
of meaning by the contrasts that are introduced. In irony we are underscoring the
more interesting features of a literal statement in a discretely comic shape. What
we take usually to be a simple and direct report is shown to have interesting
ambiguities of meaning.

In short, there is something that is revealed in the use of irony which might
otherwise escape our attention, as I have said earlier here. It is not rare for puns
to take the form of irony. In puns we replace words with other words, it is true,
but the transfer has to reach beyond this. It lives in the double meaning which
the transfer fastens on. So irony is a good deal more that just replacing one word
for another. Consider this: "His family tree is so aristocratic, that not only is
he 'blue-blooded,' but his genes are blue too." The transfer of "jeans" into
"genes" is a surface quip, of course. But the ironic character derives from what
is implied, but not stated, in the concept abbreviation. You cannot appreciate the
pun unless you confront the implied reference. More precisely, irony deals with
the whole idea, with entire concepts that are fully formed, implicitly or explicitly.
What we do is transfer a serious or literal statement into a situation that, on the
very face of it, is self-contradictory or meaningless to underscore by emphasis
what is implicit. So, for example, Professor Gold's sober, but ironic statement
that the Psychology Department has discovered God, but that psychology will
itself be absorbed into Urban Studies, which will take over every other
department in the college, and Epstein, the student, will end up having to study
Shakespeare after all, taught by Gold of the English Department, who wanted to
do so in the first place. Can you see how this implies the insanity of the strivings
of academe? But he does not say that. With sobriety, he only implies it. I think
it safe to say that even had I not characterized this as irony at the beginning of
the previous sentence, it would not have escaped you as just that.

A point made a moment ago needs re-emphasizing. I have been arguing that
irony is more than just a matter of substituting a word for a word, or a phrase for
a phrase. That it is, in fact, a matter of contextual transference in which it is
possible to compare, either implicitly or explicitly, a purely descriptive, verifiable
statement with another statement that appears to be purely declarative but which
evidently defies such classification. (Are genes blue? Is blood?)

Now, the quoted segment of Heller's novel, on the face of it, might sound as
if the professor was making a prediction in light of his understanding of the inner

workings of that college where he teaches. But even then, his statements would be predictions that would be testable sooner or later. But if one reads the whole novel, the full force of irony comes forth. Gold is a professor of English who is tormented by yearnings for fame, for success, for great wealth. He comes from a family which scorns his small achievements. He is frustrated with his wife, and longs for greater freedom as a kind of intellectual buccaneer, lover, maker of great decisions, who would earn vast amounts of money for his ability to invent startling and trenchant phrases for those in positions of great power than even he would have.

In this context, the whole discussion with Epstein reflects those frustrations, his despair, his bitterness. You know that he is deriding the college and all who teach and all who come to study there. He is saying one thing, but can you doubt that he is implying something quite different? He is saying, in his final comment in the quotation, that Urban Studies will soon take over the entire structure of the curriculum, and that every other department will become a subdivision of it. What he means is that academic structuring is lunatic. But you do not say that about your own colleagues -- at least not openly and angrily. You say it so indirectly as to appear almost as if you are not saying it at all. Doing this with finesse allows him to deny that this is what he actually meant; the students just misconstrued his statements. On the other hand, the author shows no such restraints. Internally, the work is ironic; externally, the work is an unabashed farce.

PATHETIC FALLACY

There is a sixth kind of metaphor which needs to be explained. There are several other names by which this particular type of metaphor is known. It is sometimes identified as personification, sometimes anthropomorphism, but I will stick to pathetic fallacy because the name has a more striking force. The French philosopher, Pierre Fontanier, has distinguished among three such levels of pathetic fallacy. He has said that (1) sometimes we use the animate world to metaphorize the inanimate; (2) sometimes we employ the inanimate to metaphorize the animate world, or some aspect of it; (3) sometimes we use one level of the inanimate world to metaphorize a higher level of that inanimate world. For the first, we may consider, as Wordsworth did, of stones that speak sermons to use of God's great wonder. For the second, we may say of a man that he has the intelligence of a worm-eaten block of wood. And for the third, we may say with Shakespeare, that in his flight of fancy, the poet gives locus to airy nothings.

On the face of it, metaphors, especially such as these, always edge the mind toward absurdity. It is this absurdity that appears to make the term "pathetic fallacy" so appropriate. For it is, after all, a pathetic mistake to give to inanimate matters the qualities and the traits of animate things. In literal, testable terms, for example, could anything be more absurd than to believe that "the Word takes on flesh, and the flesh becomes God"? That when Jesus said, upon breaking the bread, "This is my body, take it and eat." And on pouring the wine, adding, "This is my blood, take it and drink." Read literally, this is not only absurd, it is kind of grisly. But to fail to see its metaphoric intention, to misunderstand the symbolic intention of the ceremony of the Mass, is to fail to understand the genius of the concept of Christian tradition of the transformation from one quality of existence to a higher level.

It is often argued that the only place for the pathetic fallacy is to be found in poetry. And the truth would appear to be that this is where it is most often found, but not exclusively. If it were, it could readily be dismissed as the special domain of imagistic or symbolic poets who promote "unrealistic" dreaming. But the scientists are no less the users of this type of metaphor than the poets are, and for purposes that go in the direction of greater understanding of either the animate or the inanimate worlds. The line between science and poetry is crossed when we recognize that each undertaking is concerned with the creation of imagery. Small wonder, then, that Niels Bohr, will write that "When it comes to atoms, language can be used only as in poetry." For there appears to be no other way of describing facts sought than creating images. Either we must create catechresis to overcome an important lack, or we invoke the pathetic fallacy to transfer qualities to unexpected places. We choose the latter more often because of the power of imagery that is made possible. This will take some explaining, and good deal of justifying, to be sure.

Given our usual, familiar regard and attitude toward the magical, so to speak, and mysterious wonders of science, it is not going to be enough to quote even the most illustrious of scientists in order to make a connection between science and poetry. On the face of it, the scientist's primary concern is almost totally opposite in intention and in modes of expression to that of the poet. But that does not mean that we should disregard the examination of pathetic fallacy in the sciences. The most obvious example that comes to mind is that of Darwin's theory of natural selection. Recalling your biology, this theory states that those species that are best able to survive in a changing environment will, and that nature selects those populations of organisms that are most fit. Now, what Darwin has done here is ascribe almost human-like qualities to the environment, since it is nature's directing force that *selects* those populations of organisms that will and will not survive. Now, can the environment select as you are able to select a meal from a menu or a pair of jeans from a clothing rack? This animate quality was seen by Darwin as a means of explaining the events that he observed.

I suspect that nothing so demonstrates the protean character of metaphor as this particular form does. In the development of an effective pathetic fallacy, anything can be used to construct a metaphor for anything: horses for roses, idiots for saints, generals for pilgrims, deserts for churches, flutes for fables. Each is a potential basis for a new wondering about the world. If there is imagination enough, we can see old matters in the strangest and most unexpected new ways in the most familiar faces.

The point is, how does one cope with the unfamiliar, the unmet, the unexpected? What is there to be said of matters we have never encountered before, but which demand some explanation of us? How shall we treat what we known nothing about as yet? What is there in the world of our acquaintance that will make it possible for us to at least approach the unapproachable? What can we say of the all too familiar that will expose some aspects we had not until now even though of, even suspected? Well, whatever it is we can and do say, we say in the terms of that which is even more familiar, from which we can transfer, in some unexpected ways, to what we are seeking to learn, or to learn more about. This is the remarkable thing about the making and using of metaphor, especially pathetic fallacy. In a sense, it is very much like mixing colors on a pallet which one has never mixed before, and discovering unsuspected colors or new tones that we had never before used. And afterward, realizing that the new color is determined by the characteristics that are intrinsic to the original colors which we had used for the mixing. The new color does not arise out of nothing. It comes from the structure and features of those colors that we have just used. So too with the making of the metaphor. The unexpected meanings arise out of the meanings of the familiar terms and sentences which are being used in that transfer.

OXYMORON

One other aspect of metaphor needs to be examined so that we might introduce yet another of its types. Psychologically, as metaphors are created and used, there is produced a satisfaction from the transference of one context to another. We perceive, however unconsciously, that the metaphor fits nicely and provides an adequate way of seeing one thing as something else. So we accept the notion of the "drama of history," since the very use of that metaphor produces in us an anticipation of what will follow from seeing history as drama. If successful, the metaphor, carried out to its logical conclusions, will indeed produce a completely satisfying and delightful perception of history.

There is another type of metaphor whose purpose it is to do just the opposite: to create, however temporarily, a tension from the very juxtaposition of words. This is oxymoron. In this type of metaphor, two seemingly disparate terms are brought together to produce a new perspective, a new imagery. Thus, the "lively dead" or "thunderous silence" provides a new viewpoint that otherwise would not be available in ordinary, literal language.

The example that you have probably heard most often of oxymoron is "jumbo shrimp." The tension here is between the words that indicate that something is both large and small at the same time. But on closer examination, this may not be oxymoronic at all. Consider that the crustaceans we call shrimp were named for the features they possess. They are at once both small and curved, shriveled up. From a Middle English word, this seems to be an example of synecdoche, something being named for a feature or features possessed. But down through the years the word "shrimp" has also come to connote smallness, usually in a disparaging manner. Thus, in its original meaning, "jumbo shrimp" is not oxymoronic, but in its present connotation, it is. What does oxymoron do for us that other metaphors cannot? As mentioned, the juxtaposition of the words creates a tension of ideas, seeing something in the context of its antonym. This tension produces an imagery that brings new perspectives by providing a watershed of ideas by which new visions can be made. Like irony, oxymoron can illicit humor. Those who say that they have planted themselves firmly in midair suggests an oxymoronic condition, or a person, missing a question in the game of "Trivial Pursuit," might claim, "Oh, that's not important trivia." Are there times when an oxymoron will work (that is, produce the kind of tension and imagery we wish) and when it will not? Of course. Like any use of metaphor, there are some attempts which are successful and some which are less than so.

Let me examine two movies to illustrate how a misplaced oxymoron could produce disastrous results or very successful tension. A few years ago, a delightful movie called *Field of Dreams* told the story of a man who, upon hearing voices urging him to do so, constructs a baseball field in the middle of his cornfield. Upon completion, the ballfield becomes haunted by the spirits of oldtime professional ballplayers, including "Shoeless" Joe Jackson of the 1919 Chicago White Sox. Our protagonist believes that the sole purpose of building the field was to meet these players and watch their scrimmages. But the irony here is that he had not built for the players directly, but so that he can be reconciled with the spirit of his father, a man he could never again say that he loved. What makes this movie so satisfying and delightful is the baseball context which is used as a metaphor for the interaction among people, even the dead. Baseball is leisurely, set in a pastoral scene, with no time limits like other team sports. In that sense, the relationships of the people to the spirits of the past are also timeless; that the "game" of knowing and loving people transcends even time. The metaphor of baseball permits the father and son together to finish the business left undone, to say what had to be said, to play catch one more time. "It," as Yogi Berra has said, "ain't over till it's over."

Is there an oxymoron here? Probably not. At least the oxymoron is not readily apparent in what I have discussed above. But I do offer this to suggest something different. What would have been the result if, instead of a baseball theme, the writer had used a football one instead? Can you see how using a football metaphor to produce the same results would have been disastrous? Football is a contact sport, essentially violent in nature. There is a specified time limit place on its playing. Players are "hidden" underneath padding and helmets. To see the tender, unfinished business between a father and son in the context of the violence and time constraints of football would not have been an effective use of oxymoron.

Can oxymoron work using a football motif? Perhaps not in this above example, but in another movie it does succeed beautifully. The movie, *Brian's Song*, is about the growing friendship between two Chicago Bears football players, Gale Sayers and Brian Piccolo: a story of two men, one shy, the other outgoing; one African-American, one White; one healthy, the other dying. As running backs, the team decides that these two should room together, the first time in NFL history that players of different color shared the same room. Dispersed among the scenes of the growing friendship there are clips of actual NFL footage of Sayers and Picollo. And so we see the juxtaposition of the violence of football with the growing caring and deep concern that each has for the other. The visual oxymoron of "tender violence" works extremely well here since the tension produced between the scenes of friendship and the scenes of violent contact (especially for running backs) provides a wholly satisfying image.

One would think, I am sure, that oxymoron finds its greatest use in poetry, and that would be a correct assessment. The images produced by the constructive tension of words give the poet a new perspective to express feelings, emotions, and inner states. But because oxymoron creates such contradictory images, one might suppose that it has no place, say, in the natural sciences. If you have been following my thesis carefully, you would have to conclude that just the opposite is true, since no discipline is restricted from the use and variety of metaphors that can be used. During the first quarter of this century, physicists were in a quandary about which theory on the nature of light to accept. More traditional scholars adhered to the older wave theory. Newer "upstarts" looked at the same data and proposed that light was composed of discrete particles, called photons. It was Neils Bohr who invented his concept of "complementarity" that proposed that physics accept a dual nature of light, the wave-particle theory. This is an obvious example of oxymoron since we are asked to perceive light propagation in the contradictory metaphors of both continuous waves and discrete particles.

Some Reconsiderations

What I need to point out now is that there is no predetermined limitation placed on what can be used to transfer into a new context, to invent, or arrive at meanings in a new, heretofore unmet or undiscovered matter or a previously conceived situation. There may well be the tendency to resist transferring the inanimate onto animate matters, or animate powers and functions onto inanimate events. But depending on what we are seeking, this limitation may only be a "mental block" established by a forgotten, yet still present convention. It is deterrence by rigid preclassification, and a refusal to take the world itself and its potentiality into account. It is like arguing that one cannot mix apples and oranges. But when can we not mix apples and oranges? I can think, and I am sure you can too, of all sorts of reasons for mixing them, if we develop the category to serve the purpose. Certainly, if I can be concerned to measure or to comment on the more general classification of fruits (such as hue, skin texture, etc.), then "mixing apples and oranges" is not only legitimate, it can be fruitful. (I could not resist the pun!)

Yet when we address clichés, we come upon an aspect of the use of metaphor that must be considered. It occurs with the employment of the pathetic fallacy more than with any other. We have little difficulty in recognizing cliché. In the simplest of terms, a cliché is a metaphor which has been used so often that its original character of transfer has long since been forgotten, and the metaphor itself has become treated as an obvious truth which has become a small truism (though it is not). It is not so much the fact that it is a foolish truism that concerns us, but the fact that its constant usage marks the absence of thinking. It is a form of mindless babble, invoked on occasions when we no longer are able to be alert to the demands of intelligence. What this recognition underscores is the far more important fact that it presents us with the opportunity to construct a new metaphor, the opportunity to reach beyond the ordinary situations in which we find ourselves to make choices from the unlimited range of possibilities that lie before us, that gives added forces to the metaphorizing act. It is this possibility that shows the process of making metaphors to be the core of the thinking act.

I want to remind you that there is primary condition which must be taken into account in this business of metaphor invention and metaphor use. That condition is a vision of the universe that may very well fly in the face of all received knowledge, of all we have been reared to believe. An understanding of the range of mental activities which are made possible by metaphor invention and use leads to conclusions that the "world out there" is neither fixed nor static, nor absolutely a determinate combination of fixities interacting with one another according to "iron laws of nature." The world may not even have a *nature* in advance of our observing it. It comes to have a nature when we identify it as such. Indeed, what we come to call the "nature of humans" and the "nature of nature" depend on the tools we use to explore the external world. It is language which we possess or invent that classifies or categorizes the events of the world. The concepts that are available to us, or that we construct, are invoked to serve as the logical bases for the classifications and the distinctions that we come to agree upon. But as I have been at great pains to point out in the earlier chapters, this is an assumption that does not get itself accepted very easily, especially by stern realists who invariably argue that one cannot get far in exploring the universe, if we do not begin with the assumption that there is a reality "out there" to be explored; that that reality does not depend upon our perceptions for the character and the functions that it possesses. So you must be reminded that from this very early stage the whole question of the uses and the force of metaphor is debatable. It requires strong logical and empirical argument and demonstration, as well as justification for it to hold up. It requires, as I have said, a good deal of courage to face up to a view of the world as indeterminant and momentarily unpredictable. It also takes a great sense of humor to be able to take advantage of such an approach, especially in the face of such sternfaced and unsmiling opposition. It takes a sense of the joys, not only of discovering, but of inventing concepts that may, on the face of it, and in light of what has come be conventional beliefs, smacks of complete foolishness or outright absurdity.

Summary

Let me end this long chapter by reexamining the conditions that make metaphor not only possible, but necessary. I think I have shown that metaphor is the means of approaching, of giving identity and meaning to the unobservable, even when we have observable events in front of us. But metaphor, as an idea, performs a function not envisioned in a merely rhetorical game. Thus, I offer seven conditions within which the metaphor becomes the thinking act of the natural sciences, the social sciences, the arts, the humanities, and plain, ordinary, everyday common sense. Let me distill these for you:

(1) We sometimes see surface resemblances between what we already know and what we do not know. Now, the latter is not-yet-known because it has not yet been satisfactorily observed. So we project an analogy between the two in order to get on with investigation. We see new relationships in what the analogy permits us to see.

(2) We have available to us some single feature, or some coherent set of singular features and we give meaning to a whole complex of events in the terms of the one that is readily observable that we have in some way determined is central or essential. I have identified this as synecdoche. But it is important to note that the singular feature may not always be physical. Just as often it might be psychological, or moral or aesthetic. As when we characterize the whole individual as Dickens characterized Uriah Heep, as a craven, "oily" conniver.

(3) Sometimes, either out of perversity, from a sense of humor, or from mere curiosity, we invent what appears to be the accepted order of things in the world. Then we see what others call the cause as an effect, and the effect as a cause. The result can sometimes be quite startling, even disconcerting.   This is metonymy. As a single example here let me point out an illustration that is still used in certain parts of the world. In the age-old efforts to achieve complete harmony and symmetry among races and religions, those who argue for a "natural inequality among the races" will begin with the assumption that it is the native, perhaps genetic condition of some races, that make them inferior to other races. Turn this about and what do we get? Something like this: what these people consider to be the cause of inferiority is rather the effect of the insistence that some races must be inferior to others, in order to provide the universe with some sort of perverse symmetry.

(4) Sometimes we have no word at all to identify a new, unfamiliar event or function which we are seeking to understand. In our gropings we sometimes deliberately borrow a term from a context in which it has been especially effective and meaningful. Or we use a borrowed, effective term in place of an ineffectual term. This, as I have shown, is catechresis. Behavioral psychology, finding such terms as "soul," "spirit," even "mind," of little use in an empirical sense, has borrowed the language of mechanics and thus given totally different characteristics and functions to what was originally identified by the earlier use of that word.

(5) We have already devoted much space to the pathetic fallacy, so I need not repeat that here, except to say that this type allows envisioning a continuity between all things in nature, animate and inanimate, which we do not otherwise have.

(6) There are times when, for purposes of persuasion, for emphasis and de-emphasis, for disturbing the security of the overly secure, we employ irony. We say things which, on the face of it, have one meaning, but in the context of a larger concern, turn out to be the very opposite of the original, meaning. When it is employed without the knowledge that it is being used, it turns out to be a seriously mistaken anthropomorphism. In this way, without knowing we are doing it, we have given human powers to subhuman forms, and vice versa. We have transformed good irony into a pathetic fallacy of identification.

(7) And finally there are times when we wish to create a tension in our words, in our visual images to produce a watershed of imagery to force together two seemingly opposite things, emotions, qualities that can result in newer, richer ideas. This is oxymoron.

A word of warning needs to be made clear here about the classification I have made. Not everyone agrees that metonymy or synecdoche, for example, are types of metaphors. Indeed, they treat each of these as quite different cognitive operations, and perhaps with some justification. But I have chosen to suggest a major *class* of such cognitive activities on a rather simple notion. I am suggesting that any time we treat or perceive one event as another, we are creating and using metaphors.

Now, these are far wider conditions which make the uses and the inventions of metaphor genuine necessities, if the act of thinking is to occur. It has nothing to do with pretense, with intellectual inadequacy, with abysmal ignorance. Rather, it begins with an awareness of limitations in our knowledge of the world, of ideas and the world of things, and emerges as the activity of expanding what knowledge we do have, of shoring up intellectual inadequacies when we become aware of them in the world of direct experience. I submit that there is nothing that we do that could serve as an alternative way of thinking about the world and ourselves.

5.

MODELS AND THEIR

METAPHORIC BASIS IN THINKING

If you have ever had to put together a jigsaw puzzle, assembled a bicycle, put together a video cassette recorder so that it would operate correctly, or even repaired a mechanical instrument which has stopped operating you will already have experienced the function of a model.

We all know, however, that we do not always need a model before us to get something working or to properly "envision" what something will look like when worn or when operating. But if we want to be certain, then we do call upon some model. This is nothing more than the acknowledgement that we, most of us, paradoxically rely on vision, on actually seeing things, than on the power of the mind to cope with what we cannot see, either for the moment or at some future time. The curious thing about this, however, is that even though we do not always have an actual, tangible model before us, even when we are using what we might call "pure thought," we do indeed have a model in mind, and it is from this that we proceed in a controlled and planned way. We have, in some way, conceptualized previous events into a model of operations and we proceed by constant reference to it. For without this, all our actions are merely trial and error or, even worse, random.

The Necessity for Models in Thinking

Of course, we need to return to our central question of thinking again at this point. I have just said that even if we do not have an actual model in front of us, even when we operate on "pure thought" to choose a dress, fix a radio, write a term paper, repair a bicycle, we are still being directed, even determined, by some model which we have in mind. Now, how in the world could we ever prove this? Simply, we cannot. Then why make a point of it? Why insist on this notion? After all, is this "mind" of ours an envelope that we slide things into and from which we summon up thoughts at will? Is it a screen or a blank slate which have had things written on it and which these inscriptions can be revived at will? And what of will? All the evidence that we have and all the evidence that we know we do not have suggest that, as a series of literal statements, these are sheer nonsense.

Then what do such statements mean? It means simply that we cannot even talk about mind except in metaphoric terms, just as we cannot talk about the intricacies of modern science except in metaphoric terms. The very term "model" which is the subject of this chapter, is itself a metaphor whose purpose it is to allow us to use some aspect of the material world for purposes of talking with some possibility of clarity about the immaterial world. So we must remember when we speak of models, and of models which are "kept in mind," we are not speaking of literal events. I suspect that even at this stage of our knowledge we do not truly know how the mind contains images or memories that can be summoned up in some remarkable way. The more recent explanations of mind encoding and decoding electrochemical signals as we learn and respond to stimuli do not really answer the very simple, but profound question: *what is mind?*

I know that it can be disconcerting to students who have anticipated being taught great ultimate truths about all sorts of things in all sorts of fields that people have explored. But try to persuade yourselves that any view, which you have been asked to accept, is itself a matter of agreement among searchers who had no other way of proving their dearest dreams and hopes. An amusing alternative to this long-prevailing view was introduced earlier in the Twentieth Century by a social philosopher named Otto Neurath who likened (used a metaphor) our wanderings through the intricacies of the world to a ship floating endlessly on the high seas. Every once in awhile some of the boards of the ship would begin to weaken and rot, and need to be replaced. But there is no firm land on which to beach the ship in order to replace the rotting boards with firmer ones (that is, replacing the weakening truths with more absolute ones). All we can do is try to replace them with others, which we also have on board, without putting the ship into drydock. This is a fine example of replacing one metaphor (the metaphor of absolute truth) with that of temporary replacements of impermanent, weakening underfootings. Pick your own metaphor, always remembering that you have only exchanged one metaphor for another. Neither of them, however, is made of impermeable cement. If the metaphor is accepted, that is, if it becomes accepted by others, there are several points to bear in mind. First, used widely enough and frequently enough until it becomes an article of great familiarity, it becomes a cliché, and its origins forgotten. At that point, it takes on a reality-like character. We become easily persuaded to believe that we are actually talking about an empirical or a demonstrable fact of nature. You have to look a little more carefully at the concept to determine if indeed it can be proven to be a fact. For example, the notion that the mind is a blank slate has been so much a part of our ordinary conversation and thinking about the mind since the 17th Century, that methods of teaching you have been determined by it: teachers try to "imprint" knowledge on the minds of their students.

The second point to remember is this matter of agreement. Now, there are matters that we come to agree on that do turn out to be factual on further exploration.   But we need to sort out these situations from the kinds of agreements about which no evidence could ever be developed. Such agreements are of a different kind. Their purpose is to enable us to get on with an analysis. Whatever later conclusions we reach will always have the tentativeness that its primary agreements were based upon. They are the conclusions which result from the logical outcome entailed in the assumptions with which we began. Those assumptions, formed out of primary metaphors, will always remain just assumptions, never realities. The importance of this lies in the fact that it is a contradiction to the widely held view that a metaphor, used often enough, becomes transformed into a fact, a reality, a demonstrable statement. Unhappily, however, metaphors have no such career. They do not become transformed into facts any more than a crumb of bread transforms itself into an insect under the proper conditions of heat, humidity and nutrition.   Metaphors always remain metaphors, the act of seeing one thing in the form of another, the framework of another, envisioned as having the features of something that is more familiar to us, for purposes of explaining what needs to be explained. Crumbs may attract insects, but they do not become insects. In an analogous way, metaphors may illuminate realities, but they themselves do not become realities.

Coming back now to the matter of models, which are the overt forms we give the abstract metaphors which we have either chosen or invented, a whole new arena opens before us. If these are used to make the difficult, the confusing, the undefined apparent to us in clear, defined forms, and if they give to vision the means for more effective perception, then they are a good deal more than just tricks or tactics for dealing with complexities.

The Structure of Models

First of all, it must be noted that models come in all sizes, in many forms, making possible the performance of a variety of mental or intellectual operations. So it is imperative that we consider how models are constructed, how they are tested, what characteristics they have, how they are altered, replaced or improved. Above all, we need to know the basis for the construction of models. For the more we know about such things, the less likely we are to confuse the models with the things that are being modelled, a confusion which leads to the most absurd of consequences.

To begin with, the most obvious requirement of a model would appear to be that in some way it resembles that which is being modelled. If we can be assured that this resemblance is not only within the model, but that it is faithful to the matter being modelled, a great deal of security follows our efforts. The trouble, however, is that this matter of resemblance is a tricky one indeed. If the object we are trying to model is itself observable then the model can indeed be tested by its resemblance to that thing. But in that case, why do we need a model in the first place? Why not simply address oneself to the thing? It is the answer to this that reveals the primary need for models. For if the thing is all that observable and can be examined directly in its details, then the fact is that a model is indeed not needed. But things have histories, contingencies, potentialities, consequences and relationships which are part of the thing itself, and which must be taken into account if they are to be explained, to be given a fuller account, now and in its predicted states. In everything that we experience there are elements which we suspect may exist but which are not readily observable. The only time, then, that we do not need a model is when we do not need to explain something to ourselves or to others. Are there such moments within our lives? Of course there are. When we do not need to explain anything, when all we do is enjoy something for its own sake, revel in its presence, so to speak, then something else can be noted. We are not even required to think at all. We need only savor the moments, concerned neither with the past nor the future of the thing. But the moment we are called upon to transcend the moment beyond the immediate pleasure or pain, into the conditions of the thing, the possible alternatives to events, to causes and conditions, then we need to have before us in some active form more than the event itself provides us within its self-sustaining immediacy. So we construct a model of that thing, and project into that model aspects that the thing does not explicitly contain.

The purpose of the model, then, is to make possible observations, explorations and predictions which reach beyond the immediacy of the thing as it is presented to us. In such cases then a model will contain evidence of what is present before us and much that is not present, but whose existence we conjecture as being either possible, probable or unverifiable for the moment or at any time in the future. The most obvious matters that require models for inquiry are those things that are too small to be observed directly. The next most obvious are those things which are too large or too far away or surround us so ubiquitously as to have no definition which the senses can detect directly. Examples of each of these are not difficult to point out. To examine the inner structure of a flea, for instance, we need to enlarge the insect in whatever way is available to us.

We can do this with a high power microscope. If it is always in motion, we can employ a strobe light to slow down the action so it can be observed. When things are too large, we employ instruments which will diminish their size while keeping structures intact. If they are too distant, we use instruments which will bring them close enough for more direct examination. If their definition is indiscernible to the immediate senses, we could employ chemical tests to separate their aspects and provide us with definition that way.

In every such case, we recognize that, by means of some instrument, we have constructed an object that resembles the original, but is not the original itself. It has become a model of that object, no matter how exact the resemblance between the modelled thing and its model. And by means of the model we can probe into things that the things themselves do not permit. In the enlargements or reductions we are able to conjecture about aspects of its existence which things in themselves do not permit us to do. There is a sense, however in which this kind of model is the most obvious one to construct. There are aspects of the model which are hardly simple, and which we will come to shortly, in the effort to show its fuller complexity, and the quite remarkable functions they enable us to perform. It is when we come to other kinds of models that the fuller functions of models are revealed as irreducible supports for the act of thinking. When we try to analyze theories, doctrines or what we call "pure concepts" in verbal or linguistic forms, then both the difficulties in constructing models and the functions they permit us to perform become evident.

Consider the wristwatch that you are wearing. Some of you have watches in which the face is marked out in a circle, bearing the numbers one through twelve, and hands that mark off seconds, minutes, and hours. Some other watches will have blank faces in which numbers appear in sequence giving the moment in time. Both are models of the flow of something that we call time. The former is called an analogue watch, and is a model of the movements of celestial objects. The latter is called a digital watch, and is a mathematical model of time seen as numerical sequences measured in digits. The curious thing about both is that they are models of what cannot be seen. That is, they do not measure time, but something else used to represent time. It is not very difficult to see why the models, in these cases, become the events being modelled. Time becomes, in reality, what the watch tells you it is. But the differences in the watches should intrigue you, for it ought to raise the question: what is time, *really*? The illustration that each gives is a relationship between a model of something and the thing that is modelled. As you might realize, these are not in the least simple. In fact, in this case, each watch is a model of an entirely different thing. The digital watch is a model of a mathematical measurement which we use to separate periods of the day. The analogue watch is a model of the apparent movement of the sun across the sky every day. "Ten minutes to one" and "12:50" refer to the same undergirding conception of time in passage. The language, however, is so different that for an innocent mind the one says something that is incomprehensible in terms of the other. If you think that this is odd, let me tell you that I once gave a digital watch to a boy who was used to only telling time according to an analogue watch. He returned it to me the next day, saying that he did not like it because he could not read it. Could I give him the other kind of watch? For him at least, though he never actually said anything like that, it was obvious that time was what a familiar type of watch said it was. The model, you see, was the thing that was being modelled.

Types of Models

But let me move from this simple example to more difficult ones. I hope to show you that, in actuality, our whole lives are determined by the models which organize the world for us, giving it meaning and direction. Briefly, then, here are some types of models.[1] The *analogical* model provides a means to perceive, in some observable way, something else which is not directly observable. A *scale* model, like a map or a blueprint, provides us with a larger or smaller view of some physical features. In addition, we might point to a photograph as a *representative* model, for the picture represents that which it is a picture of. The model that has come down to us of the structure of the atom is an example of a *theoretical* model, for it gives us a visual form to something which has neither form nor content to the naked eye. When we diagram a sentence or when we give description to the structure of a written work, say of a novel, we are offering a *linguistic* model. When we balance our checkbook, work out a geometry proof or apply a statistical analysis to some set of events, we are using a *mathematical* model.

Each of the six kinds of models here are, in fact, models of different kinds of events which we experience daily. So that one important thing to be said of models is that there are always ways we can organize a wide range of matters which we experience. To be able to keep them apart is to be able to keep separate elements of our experiences. And to be able to do that is to be enabled to distinguish between fact and theory, between dream and reality, between what is and what is desired, among what is, what was and what might be.

---

[1]

For a more complete description of models, see Mary Hesse (1966) and Max Black (1962).

There is another familiar way of distinguishing models. The terms *hard*, *soft*, and *mixed* are words that are quite familiar to us. While the categories identified above refer directly to the form of the model, these three refer to the things and events being modelled. A hard model is a model of actual, determinate matters which can be seen and handled directly to some degree. A soft model is a model of what cannot actually be seen or touched or peered into -- matters like feelings, motivations, ideas. And mixed models are models in which we combine what can be peered into with matters which only have existence in symbolic form. Thus, we call the materials we examine and experiment with in the natural sciences the substance of hard models. The subject matters of the arts, like poetry, music, drama, painting, and dance, can be classified as soft models. The social sciences are developed into mixed models, for they are models resulting from the mixing of hard evidence and feeling states, concepts, desires, anticipations and the like.

What we attempt to model, however, cannot be taken too simply. This fact will cause us a great deal of difficulty, if not outright confusion. For the matters of the world as we perceive them are already clothed so that we can see them. The philosopher Immanuel Kant insisted that without some already existing concepts which we "have in mind" we have only empty perceptions of the things of the world. Many have pointed out, scientists, philosophers, and psychologists, that we see what our concepts allow us to see, and that these concepts actually precede the act of seeing, although they may have been built out of experiences of the past. We see then events of the world, even the world itself, given form and meaning with the concepts that we use to clothe that world, however specific or general. The concepts themselves, it is reminded, are based on some metaphors which make them functional. In this way, we may recognize the connection between the metaphors which give meaning and structure to our experiences, and the models which make it possible to explore, experiment and explain those experiences.

It must be understood that all of this is not simply a psychological aberration. It is, rather, an epistemological matter, a statement about the way knowledge functions in the human mind. As such, it must be treated as purely hypothetical, not as a scientific fact.

Again, the question of what in the world we can depend on in such situations, must arise. And the answer is, as it was before, on mutual agreement that one hypothesis or another is worth working out in greater detail, to see where it will lead us, what conclusions it can offer, and what consequences can arise from such conclusions. So the metaphors themselves are not scientific substances, but the products of scientific minds that attempt to make sense of the external world. Between what I have called the primary experiences and the secondary experiences, the employment of the latter provides us with the verbal and symbolic means of organizing, explaining and describing the former. The models which we develop can either be models of direct experience or models for discourse. Kept in mind, this difference makes it possible for use to avoid confusing the two realms: what we say about the world from the world itself. The importance of this distinction cannot be overemphasized. For we are always in danger of that most deadly of all metaphoric mistakes; confusing thinking with what that thinking is about, making concrete what is only verbal, confusing the model of something for the thing itself. In doing this unwittingly, or unconsciously, we are guilty of unguarded metonymies or ridiculous pathetic fallacies.

With this in mind, let me come back to the types of models which are available to us, and to the thinking functions that they make possible. I have already mentioned two different ways of distinguishing model types. I have classified them as hard, soft, and mixed models. I have also discussed, although briefly, about scale models, representative models, analogical models, mathematical models, linguistic models and theoretical models. If you bring the two together, you will find that they illuminate each other. Representative, mathematical or scale models are hard, since they are concerned to redescribe the tangible matters of the world in forms and structures that can be handled. Analogical models are clearly soft for a number of reasons. There is no requirement of resemblance or similarity of physical features in analogical models. Rather, the purpose of an analogical model is to see the relationships of one event in terms of the relationships of another event. So, for example, and a most absurd one at that, we decide to use a cake of ice as a model to describe the character of a political figure. Obviously, we are not referring to the physical features of either the ice or the politician. What we are referring to are the qualities and relationships that are associated with the cake of ice that are now used to describe the qualities of the individual person whom we are addressing. It is important to note that the choice of this model does not involve any specific external or factual evidence. It depends on a speculative set of qualities being applied to unexpected events or persons.

The third forms, theoretical and mixed models both involve combinations in varying degrees of actual data to be explored and are explained along with speculations about unobservables which are assumed to exist, and whose presence then provides us with the basis for such explanations. That is what we mean by mixed, and this too is essential to theoretical models. I think that you can see that each of these three models have different characteristics, different sources, perform rather distinctive functions and are tested in different ways precisely because they have different origins and different dependencies. I think, too, that you can anticipate which of the various disciplines that you will be encountering will be using which of these models. In a rough sort of way, we can guess that the natural sciences will require the use of hard and scale models since what we are dealing with in these sciences are the rough data of the external world. To do so, we will be called upon to construct models of things as they actually exist. The social sciences, with their much larger and more tenuous range of concerns and qualities will very likely oblige us to use mixed models, while the arts and the humanities will be engaged with soft models, expecting to reflect qualities of feeling states, of emotions, of intentions, of flights of fancy.

If only the distinctions could be so easily and so cleanly maintained! But troubles assail us all too quickly when we realize that the hard sciences are *theory-born* and *theory-bound*. The soft models rely on experiences with actual things in the world, and depend upon our ability to locate those things within the symbols which form the models. For mixed models, the problem here is how much of the model reflects actuality and how much theory. Is there a formula to be used that will help us determine whether we have slipped from a mixed model to one of the other two models? Unhappily, no. More often than not, something which we call intuition is at work here; the leap of imagination which appears to transcend the neat progress of slow logic. To be stated more simply, hard models will always be compromised, not only by the actual events and materials examined, but also by the theoretical concepts which we assume "hold together" those events. These will not have the concreteness that we would expect a hard model to contain. Soft models, if we take the arts as illustrative, invariably refer to things of the world which are being transformed into symbols of feeling states. An El Greco figure, for example, however elongated, is still a figure which we can recognize for all its distortions. And of mixed models, we need only point out that the terms themselves indicate that there is always an amalgam of the actual and theoretical involved.

Models and Types of Explanations

Does that mean, then, that the terms hard, soft, and mixed are useless? Hardly. It only means that we must be careful how we use them, what we apply them to, and what we need to look for in them. From each, more briefly, we can expect a different function and a different outcome. From hard models we expect a conclusion or an explanation that will stand the scrutiny of a community of inquirers who will finally agree on the claims made. From soft models we will be looking for images which will stir in us some understanding and some personal recognition in our own lives. From mixed models, the theoretical explanations will give meanings to data which derive, not from the data alone, but from the data as organized by certain assumptions. And such outcomes will not have the certainty of hard models or the image-creating qualities of the soft. Thus, the names given to the various models are intended to direct expectations of outcomes, not to describe the characteristics of the models themselves, and then to suggest the kinds of conclusions we can make from the use of these models.

As important as it is to make clear the differences between models in terms of the types of explanation we may expect from each (even to the point that for at least one type, the soft models, no explanations are expected) it is probably no less important to be clear about the distinction and relationship between models and metaphors. To this we now turn.

Distinguishing between Models and Metaphors

Models are re-descriptions of things that appear to the innocent eye. That is, no model is simply a replica of some thing, some idea or some image. It is always a reconstitution, in some way, of what is available to the ordinary observation for the deliberate purposes of exploring those things. As I have said, features are exaggerated or diminished, size is enlarged or made smaller, colors intensified, placements altered somewhat for illustrative purposes, functions or processes slowed, accelerated or halted altogether, so that they can be better observed. The descriptions given these reconstituted matters are properly re-descriptions since they will necessarily differ from those we have become used to. Even when we are dealing with the matters of what we have called soft models, the same thing happens. A painter *re-presents* a landscape in ways which surprise the rest of us. A poet *re-describes* familiar feelings and thoughts in such ways that we may find ourselves saying, "I never thought about it in that way." The social scientist will introduce an explanatory concept that obliges us to re-describe familiar data in a surprising, unfamiliar way. In each case, the re-description and/or the re-presentation gives new meaning and unexpected illumination to what has become familiar to us.

In these ways, models bring difficult or distant matters closer to us so that we can deal with them in ways that nature itself apparently does not permit. And these operations define the purposes from which models are constructed. But the trouble arises for us when we realize that these very same functions are also performed by metaphors. How, then, do we distinguish between models and metaphors, if we can distinguish them at all? The fact is that so illustrious a philosopher as Max Black has argued that they are distinguished only by what they redescribe. In his view, metaphors address concepts which identify the arts and the humanities while models are concerned with the realities of nature and human behavior. But there are, I think, more distinctions to be made than just this. Although this must first be added: there are occasions when a model can be considered a metaphor in and of itself. This could easily end us up in even greater confusion, if we fail to recognize the difference between treating the content and treating the form of a given event. I am sure this is not very revealing, but it is worth paying attention to.

Unless we have been in some way alerted to it, when we encounter things, our attention is directed to its content. That is, to what the thing is made of, and what the thing does. Perhaps the simplest illustration of this that I can give deals with seeing a play or a movie. Our attention is caught by what is transpiring on the stage or on the screen. What we follow is the story as it unfolds; what is happening, who is doing what, to whom, and finally how it all ends. So, *Hamlet* is the story of a prince whose father is murdered by his uncle, who then marries the young man's mother, and plots to kill the young prince too. But the prince is suspicious of his uncle, although he has no direct evidence, and sets about to make the uncle convict himself out of a guilty conscience. In the end, after much turmoil, most of the people in the play are killed, some justifiably, some unhappily. If we can keep the story line clear in our minds, we can claim to know what *Hamlet* is about.

It is already quite sophisticated to be able to say that *Hamlet* is a story of a man who could not make up his mind. It is even more so to be able to say that the play has a classical structure of form in terms of time, and tension and resolution. That its subjects are nobility, that it reveals us to ourselves as greater than we really are, and so on. But when we have reached the point of being able to make such observations, we have moved from a concern with the content of the play to the form or structure of it. From such observations, we move in the direction of making a generalization about the play as a whole -- as content given a particular form. What is constructed can now serve as a model for considering, analyzing, explaining or interpreting not only a specific play, in this case *Hamlet*, but other plays which we also want to analyze and interpret. So the form or structure of the play, not its content, can become a model that can be used for further explorations. By means of such a model, a whole range of further comments, analyses, interpretations of other plays is made possible.

But sometimes a play like *Hamlet* comes to be used as a metaphor too, and here confusion can arise. Used as a metaphor, we will be saying something quite different about the play or some aspect of it. Say we chose to speak of *Hamlet* as a metaphor for the "torment of uncertainty." This is quite different from saying that *Hamlet* is a model of uncertainty. Or we may choose to speak of the play, as a whole, as a metaphor for the struggle between greed and lust on one hand, against purity and innocence on the other. Again this is quite different from saying the play is a model of that struggle. The simple and obvious fact is that with metaphor we are, at least in this case, dealing with something other than physical elements and their behaviors. We are dealing with states of mind, emotions, intentions, passions. And since there are not likely to be externally observable events that can be identified with such states, we can make no universal model of them. They will differ in appearance and in quality with each individual. If, however, we were to be concerned to explore and explain the content of the play in its narrative form, showing the line of development from opening scene to the last fights, and the deaths, we might be able to construct a model of it which would then be a paradigm of Shakespearean tragedies and which could be used to anticipate and predict others of Shakespeare's tragedies.

Thus, the model addresses itself to the forms of matters, while the metaphor is a judicious transfer of familiar states to new events, to bring them into more intimate contact, and to give them external characteristics so that they can be actually observed.

If this were all that can be said about the difference between models and metaphors, it would be simple enough. The trouble is, however, that although I have considered a work of art here, the fact is this process also takes place in the natural and social sciences. Now, we all seem to agree that the arts and the sciences are totally different kinds of intellectual and emotional undertakings. As I will show in a moment, however, the creation of metaphors and models operates very similarly in these wide ranges of intellectual endeavors. But I want to recapitulate something here.

See what I have done in an effort to distinguish between models and metaphors. I have argued that when we are concerned with ostensible matters (that is, matters that in some way can be observed) from intentions (matters which cannot be observed, only inferred), we must move from matters of direct, primary experience to secondary, indirect experiences. The former are critical parts of any model which we can construct. The latter are, in effect, metaphoric in nature, because we borrow from one range of experiences to create conceptual figures of matters which are nameless or have no immediate identity. But there is one trouble that still arises, as I have already suggested. And this is that no model is exclusively made up of observable matters, and that no metaphor is without reference to some aspect of the material world. Nevertheless, this does not make them merely variations of one another, or synonymous with one another, serving in different kinds of undertakings. What is common to them is that both rely on evidence in some way, but what is uncommon between them is that they use this evidence for totally different purposes. In models, this evidence or observable material is the subject to be explained. In metaphor, this observable material is used as the basis for making assumptions, for constructing hypotheses which cannot be verified, but which provide us with the context from which we construct systems of meanings or alternate meanings to things that we know nothing about or whose meanings we are altering by further investigations. It is the fact of these different functions that both distinguish models from metaphors, and creates a sequential relationship between the two.

For models, in order to be constructed, not only require matters to be modelled, but also concepts, hypotheses, theories, assumptions which will make the construction of those models possible. It is for this reason that I have said repeatedly that models are the tangible forms we give our metaphors, and the demonstrable means for testing them for their explanatory value.

Now let me illustrate what I am talking about in the sciences, in order to provide you with the bases for my argument that thinking is thinking, whether it be in the arts, the humanities or any of the sciences. Some time in your college studies you will meet a sociological problem like demography. Simply stated, this is the statistical study of population distributions. You will be introduced not only to the data of different cultures, different races, different groups in various parts of a geographical entity, but also to the methods for discriminating such grouping. You will learn, for example, how many of a particular national, racial or ethnic group reside in a certain region. You will learn how these groups interrelate in professional arenas, in religious organizations, the kind of work they do, their level of education, and so on. In order to be able to make accurate reports, you will learn the statistical methods that have been developed for the analyses of this information so that you will be able to make statistically discriminating claims. But what your models, as models, will not enable you to explore are the basic motives, the fundamental involvement of one's beliefs, as compared to another, the limits that such beliefs impose on its adherents, and the reaction which adherents of one faith have toward other "alien" faiths. And yet, if we are ever to reach a point of being able to suggest approaches that might ease transitions from one stage of growth to another, these are matters we ought to be able to confront, to understand, certainly to identify and appreciate. Such matters, moreover, are not measurable, or manipulable by any statistical means. For all of these are rooted in the metaphors, the conventions, by which various groups live and act. It is one thing to say that such and such a group has such and such a faith, or such and such a membership in this or that grouping. It is a completely different matter to reach into these faiths, the conditions for membership, the permissiveness and limitations which membership imposes upon its members, and the conceptual grounds for whatever freedoms and whatever restraints exist to identify each of the groups. These can only be approached through analysis of the metaphors and their types which serve as the roots of belief and behavior.

In all this, there is a similarity between what constitutes sociological study and the study of a drama such as *Hamlet*. It is one thing to build a model of the way in which the drama unfolds, the narrative unrolls. It is quite another to analyze the intentions of the author or any of the characters of that drama. In the metaphoric analysis of the latter, we find ourselves going beyond the drama itself, borrowing from whatever other disciplines have to lend us, from whatever classifying sources we have become familiar with, to enable us to penetrate into the mind of Hamlet, of Ophelia, of Shakespeare.

One further, brief example of this relationship between model and metaphor, this time in the natural sciences, especially of modern physics. For those who have studied even a little atomic theory, you will recognize that the most famous model of the structure of the atom is the Rutherford-Bohr model that describes the structure of the atom along the lines of the known model of the solar system. But there is an interesting aspect to this. On first being taught this model, young people readily accept the model as being an accurate description of the way in which the nucleus holds the electrons in their proper orbits. The model becomes the event itself, and is learned as such. Whatever else is added (reactivity of elements, classifications of metals and non-metals, valence, ionic states) is learned as a report from authorities. After all, it is the chemistry teacher who says so, and he or she knows this stuff.

What the student will not see for a long time (or may never realize), are the arguments among chemists and physicists on the validity or the testability of this or that particular model. And if a student ever did hear actual discussions which go beyond a consideration of the specific model, into the disputes over what constitutes *reality* in this or that model, and whether such concepts are warranted or not, she or he would hear just how metaphors come to serve as the basis for whatever model of the atom is being debated.

What does become apparent, as I will show in Chapters Six and Seven, is that any model in any branch of science contains within it evidence of the metaphoric assumptions which contribute to the construction of the model in just the form that it is given. It is, you must realize, a metaphoric operation that motivates a physicist such as Bohr to say that the atom behaves *as if* it were an extremely small solar system.

At this point, the whole problem of hard, soft, and mixed models comes back to haunt us. We have said that if any area of study will be identified with hard models it will be the study of the sciences, because these areas deal with the things of the world, testable and demonstrable by objective means. Yet here, in this simple example, we come upon the problems of dealing with aspects of reality which are simply not observable, but which oblige us to construct observable surrogates for things we either cannot see for the moment, or may never see at all. And yet, to avoid dissolving back into the mythologies that haunted our early efforts of understanding the things of the world, we must re ognize that the natural sciences require us to stay with the idea of hard models, even if we have to redefine just what a hard model really is. So we ought to do just that: to suggest a more defensible and clearer definition of a hard model, and what can be expected of it.

A Comparison of Types of Models

When we speak of hard models, we are usually referring to what have been called scale or representative models, though this is not always the case. Both analogue models and theoretical models can also be hard. What makes them hard, as I have said, is not the form of the model alone, but what the models are supposedly models *of*. They are models of things and the way things work. They refer then to sensible matters which we are trying to learn about, to discover their so-called secrets which we can do in no other way. If this is so, then we feel better when the model actually represents the materials we are exploring, reduced or enlarged, so that we can see them better, examine them more directly, manipulate them in ways we could not manipulate the original materials. But this means that we must not be misled by the term "hard." It does not mean that by the use of hard models, we are going to be able to prove our claims. It means rather, as Paul Ricoeur has said, that the use of these models allows us to discover what we ordinarily might not even suspect exists. What scale models do especially is that they give us a security that we are in fact modelling the things that we are seeking to explore, and that the discoveries we then might come upon do indeed have relevance to matters with which we are concerned.

This is not always true of analogue models, and even less so of theoretical models. In analogue models we are dealing not with physical resemblances so much as we are with similarity of relationships. With theoretical models we are dealing with conceptual structures based on logical, rather than some actual resemblances.

But even these distinctions are not as clarifying as they appear to be. You will remember that the scale model is not mere replication or imitation of some thing in the sensible world; it is imaginatively altered for specific, exploratory reasons. Something besides physical characteristics as they exist, or relationships as they can be observed, or features as they can be recorded, say, by a camera, will have to be built into the model. There will have to be some assumptions or presuppositions that we can use to give coherence and relevance to those models with respect to what it is we are making models of. Without such presuppositions we can construct models only of what we directly see, in the actual form that we see it. But then, as I have said, we would have no need of a model in the first place. If we need a model, then we also need presuppositions and assumptions about what cannot be directly approached. And the source of those presuppositions and assumptions finally comes to us in metaphoric organizations. Thus, the role of metaphor in the construction and employment of models we use as a means of exploring, discovering, and explaining the world we live in, and the many worlds we talk about and read about.

Summary

I have argued that models are indispensable to the process of thinking, since it is models that provide us with the means to explore, observe, explain, describe or otherwise make sense of the events that we encounter everyday. We have only to place a potato in front of us to realize that we can and do bring a host of models to say something about that potato. Biologically, the potato is a tuber, a form of a root. Economically, the potato represents a crop that can be sold for profit. Historically and sociologically, the potato became an important factor in the development of Ireland and the immigration of the Irish to the United States.[2] Can you think of any other models that can be brought to the potato? I am sure that you can.

At the basis of any model, there resides a metaphor upon which the model has been constructed. For example, at the foundation of a statistical analysis of some set of events, there is the acceptance of the metaphor that those events will follow the laws and principles of mathematics that helped shape those statistical models.

---

[2]

See Harry Hobhouse's *Seeds of Change* (1986) for an examination of the role of five plants in the transformation of societies.

In a sense, then, models are metaphors that have grown up. With the initial perspective of seeing something as something else, the metaphor can grow and expand to encompass larger contexts for explanation or description, become more serviceable in its tasks, providing a tangible means to make sense of the events of the world.

Models can be classified into two types. I have identified that there are different types of models; analogical, mathematical, literary, scale, and so on. Each of these types or forms are concerned with the structure of the model itself, and not with the events modelled. In this latter case, I have distinguished among hard, soft and mixed models that refer to the events under scrutiny. Again, hard models are constructed from tangible, observable events; soft models are constructed from the intangibles of feeling states, motivations, emotions. Mixed models are just what the word suggests: models that examine events that possess elements of both intangibles and tangibles.

As you continue with or begin your college studies, you will see that what are presented to you through your readings, lectures, and discussions are the models of those various disciplines. It might even be said that to become a member of a discipline requires that you accept the models that have been invented and are used within that discipline. Further, you might have already suspected that the disciplines that you are taught are characterized by the types of models that are used within them. To this, we will become increasing specific in the next two chapters.

6.

MODEL TYPES AND

THE DISCIPLINES

In the last chapter, I introduced the concepts of the types of models which, in a sense, have "grown up" from constant use in the inquiry of nature and humans. I have identified them as hard, soft, and mixed. The first uses hard data or tangible referents as the basis of explaining behavior, growth, changes and functions in the actual world. A wave model for light, for instance, is based on both the hard data of reflection, refraction, and other observable phenomena, and represents how we think about the nature of light and its behavior. The second includes models that are given some tangible forms of those things which themselves have no tangible existence. For example, a school of art that becomes the accepted form of expression for some time. It is important to remember that, although soft models are tangible, what they refer to, what they represent and symbolize are not. And the mixed models are those in which we find tangible symbols or representations of both tangible and intangible matters. A sociological study may depend on very hard statistical analysis for its claims, but those claims are based on intangibles, such as freedom, oppression, liberty, desires, and the like.

These are models that are constructed to combine references to things and references to ideas, theories and/or feelings. I have also said that our traditions have taught us that the hard models identify the natural sciences, the soft models identify the arts, and the mixed models, combining elements of hard and soft, make possible and give form, function and direction to all the disciplines that are classified under the social sciences.

Models as Human Invention

If, as I have said, models are perceptions of what there is in the world (and in humans) and how one is to think about these, at least we can say that what we know about a given discipline, how we think within a given discipline, is determined by the very models those disciplines have made for the purpose of their inquiries and their explanatory systems. Thus, our knowledge in any given discipline is generated and filtered through the very models of that discipline. This becomes obvious when we reject the notion that whatever we can know must come exclusively from the events under examination themselves. Not knowing, for instance, what a lily flower is, someone points to one and says, "That is a lily. If you want to know anything more about it, other than the connection of a name with the thing, go ask the lily flower itself. For, after all, the lily is the producer of its own models. Study the model and you study the flower. They are one and the same thing."

What have we been doing here? You might have already guessed by now that we are ascribing very human-like qualities to our flower. No longer do we have to make sense of this event, since it is the flower itself that will tell us all. At this stage of our analysis, I think that you will agree that you will understand that no matter how much we would like to believe it, the events out there in the world do not have any meaning in and of themselves. As humans, we give meaning to them.

How valid is the example of the lily above? Quite valid, I would suppose, but with one fairly important reservation, perhaps two. In spite of these reservations, though, there is a good deal of value in the analogy.

First the reservations. I have argued that a model of something is not the thing itself. If it was, there would be no need for a model. A model lily or a model of a lily contains both more and less than the lily itself does; and it contains it in a form of concentration, organization, emphasis and de-emphasis which the flower itself does not. The *modelled form* is constructed for just those purposes and for explanation. The flower does not organize itself to teach about itself, or to explain the characteristics of its existence, its origins, growth, and reproduction. Precisely because this is so, we make a model of the flower, within which we build those aspects to be studied. And if the model is to be really instructive and explanatory, we include the possibilities of movements to shorten the normal time dimensions between origin and death, enlarge certain features for closer study, and eliminate in the model those features that do not affect our purpose of study.

This leads to the second reservation. Models are invented instruments with distinctively human purposes for making them. If we then say that the lily makes it own models, we are giving a literal connotation to a fairly obvious metaphor: giving human powers to a thing which is obviously not human. That this is done over and over again does not alter the fact that it is an example of a misused pathetic fallacy. The "voice" we hear from the flower is not the flower's at all, but our own, projected imaginatively, and received back in our own ears.

But barring these two reservations, and recognizing that we can make a model of anything in the world, and do so, either in some external form, such as a picture, a blueprint, a sculpture, or even verbally, the analogy has the persuasiveness and instructive value described above.

The point of this brief discussion, however, is of more than passing importance to us. It must be recognized that an event or an object does not tell us in what way a model must be made. These are choices that we make, and are not dictated by the object or event itself. Indeed, if you have been following my argument on the thinking process, anything can be used to symbolize anything else. We may often be led in a model to accurately imitate the shape or texture or colors of the object as we construct our model. But the thing modelled will not reach out and pull our ears if we do not do this. We can symbolize these in any way that we anticipate our own needs that will enhance our possibilities for study. But those relationships which we are seeking to explain must be symbolized in the materials that we have decided to use. Thus, a plaster model of our lily flower will necessarily possess different shapes, colors, and textures to distinguish among the petals, anthers, ovules, and stigma of the flower. But here again, not even the relationships need to be mirror reflections of the relationships in the event or object. When we consider the matter of relationships, we suddenly find ourselves, not in a tangible, easily observable realm, but in the realm of concepts or hypotheses.

The concept of causality, which is a fine instance of *relationship,* is an example of just this matter. What do we actually look for in our model to describe or report a causal relationship? Can we, returning to our lily model, really see the relationships between pollen formation, pollination of the stigma, growth of the pollen tube, fertilization of the ovules, and seed formation? No, not directly. What is needed to fill in this explanation of causal relationships or a description of sequences is someone who will carefully show how this series of steps leads to seed formation. Thus, the series of causes are cognitive constructions showing the relationships between events. You would be correct to claim, at this point, that this process of filling in the connections with less than tangible referents must surely reduce the hardness of that model. Not completely, of course, but sufficiently enough to prevent us from saying that every aspect of a hard model is a symbol of some tangible event in nature. And it is just such elements in the model that make the model a proper means for study, a proper instrument for developing explanations. If we explain what nature does not, it is because we symbolize the intangibles that nature does not make tangible or obvious for us.

The Criteria of the Tangible and Intangible

Concerning this last point, one of the most serious implications suggests that science was never as "hard" as has been claimed. That, as it has quite often been pointed out, science is never as precise as it was thought to be; never as exact as it was hoped. It is full of theories and hypotheses which appear in scientific models in tangible form, but cannot be identified with equally hard references.

If this can be said about hard models, what can we say about soft models? Much in the same vein, I suspect. That is, the arts cannot be reduced to mere fantasies, given some tangible symbols, but symbols that refer to nothing in the tangible world. That must be obvious to everyone. Paintings of trees have as their reference some aspect of these very tangible matters. If they also have reference to feeling states, or to imaginary visions, they still have trees as at least one of their referents. Even modern art, where there may not be any resemblance between the referent and what is presented on the canvas, is created to show some *thing* or some *feeling*. If a dance symbolizes the primitive concepts of worship and celebration, it still also has the human body in motion as one aspect of its referents. If a poem symbolizes "the mind brooding over a lost love," it still has human beings and concrete human features as one of its referents.

Thus, in all the arts, not even the softest model is devoid of hard or tangible references. There is always the mixture of the two here, as there is always the mixture of the two in scientific (hard) models. Perhaps, then, we are saying that all the models of all these disciplines are really refugees from the social sciences which, for the most part, frankly accept that mixture as the requirements for their kinds of inquiry. Neither is it enough to say that the distinction between all three types of discipline area is in the weighing of its referents. That is, in the natural sciences, the hard data predominates as reference; in the soft arts the imaginary, the dreamy, the inventive predominates; while in the mixed models the weight of the referents is equal. Such an argument would ask for a quantifiable measurement which regrettably could never be achieved. How, for instance, does one weigh facts against theories? How can we specify that an "X" number of theoretical statements must be built into such and such theory?

I make much of this only because so much of positivist science argues the opposite, namely, that theories and hypotheses are not really necessary for science to do its work of description and explanation. Indeed, many have said, that when all theories (and, they add, all metaphors) are replaced by facts, by the actual mirroring in our models, science will finally become fully mature. Theories and metaphors, they argue, are simply fill-ins, waiting for the new or "true" facts to arise. This is, of course, a curious view. But what primary metaphor and model of nature directs them to such a conclusion? It would be illuminating, I think, to understand the mythology that they accept, that enables them to denounce the use of theories, metaphors, and to be blunt about it, all other mythologies.

Distinguishing the Disciplines

How then shall we distinguish the models of the sciences from those of the social sciences and those of the arts in the context of the thesis presented here? You already know that sometimes the distinction is very clear, for instance, as you begin course registration. Read a course catalogue and you will see the offerings by the various departments. You would not anticipate finding an art course listed under the biology department. Further, you would be very suspicious if you read that the history professor who taught "Ancient Cultures" last year is now scheduled to teach "Elizabethan Poetry." During your junior high and senior high school days, how many times have you heard one of your fellow students admonish a social studies teacher who required proper syntax, spelling and grammar on homework assignments with the statement, "Why do we have to do this? This isn't English class!"

How then to distinguish among the disciplines? Would we be able to make greater contributions to enhancing one's ability to think by shifting the focus from materials and methods, and concentrating on purposes? Such a view is very tempting to many scholars, experimenters, and teachers. For, by breaking down the barriers erected, we eliminate those specializations which have made communication among scholars increasingly difficult. And it is generally agreed that it is very likely these methods and materials that prevent effective communication. Thus, the shifting from these to the purposes of the various disciplines needs to be examined more carefully than has usually been done.

Let us begin with an obvious fact. A collegiate majors in a given field. The degree is always accompanied by the statement of identification of that field. "I have a B.A. with a major in (history, chemistry, literature, accounting, etc.)." This identification is increasingly more restrictive at the master's and doctorate levels. These are undoubted facts. You would hardly be expected to teach literature in college when your degree is in physics.

So, any argument that such distinctions are arbitrary and meaningless in a larger educational sense, is probably an argument from desire, or from some Utopian or Garden of Eden vision than from a well-grounded set of data.[1]

For our analysis of models and metaphors, what can we say about this matter? After all, it affects the work you do in school so completely that your whole perception of yourself and the world you live in is at stake.

I know that I have taken an unconscionable long time presenting this problem to you, but I hope you will understand why I have done so. It is, after all, in the very spirit of teaching to think, which requires an increasingly precise statement of just what the problem, any problem, is; what sides there are to the problem; who says what about it and why. Otherwise, I would be guilty of doing what I charge too many others of doing: giving out statements that I pronounce as the truth and expect students to accept them without further inquiry into the origins of my claims and conclusions.

It is true that matter alone does not determine a field of study, as I have shown that many different disciplines can concern themselves with the same matter. But the matter under study needs first to be recast and reconstituted in the form of our models for the purpose of inquiry. What is studied then is not the matter in total, but some specific aspect of matter that is isolated or concentrated and made manifest through the thinking process. This suggests then that it is not so much matter that we are concerned within each of the disciplines, but the behaviors of the aspects of matter. A model, then, is always a functioning affair, a means by which we perceive, not its gross character, but the way matter functions in given, natural or constructed settings, deliberately created to actually or cognitively observe the character, range, and limitations of its behavior.

If all we had to do was to give form to something that already has form, such as a topographic map, the task would not be difficult at all. When we attempt to give form to something that we only suspect has material form (the nature of the

---

[1]

Education, I am sure you know, suffers from arguments of this disjunctive kind. One group argues from data, the other from the concepts of a new logical structure, and no agreements are ever reached, only temporary accommodations. What the latter group seems to be saying is, "Wait until we get into positions of authority! We'll turn the whole curriculum around and finally make it reasonable." And do they? Good question. I suspect it is as difficult to alter long traditions of the distinctions among the disciplines as it is to change the beliefs of anyone who has grown up, comfortably and happily, in the oddest kinds of metaphors.

If all we had to do was to give form to something that already has form, such as a topographic map, the task would not be difficult at all. When we attempt to give form to something that we only suspect has material form (the nature of the electron), that is more difficult, but not overwhelmingly so. There it is an issue of patience and logical accuracy. What is extremely complex is the task of giving some form to something that has no chance of ever being material, having specific form. How, for example, can we give form to the "Monday morning blue feeling"? There is a catch here that you may have already spotted. To suggest the word "blue" already implies something tangible -- a measurable light wave, a pigmentation. What does "blue" refer to or symbolize when discussing human feelings? It is even more complicated when this is compared to the expression of "being in the pink" which seems to have some tangible referent to skin tone in some of us.

Here then we can perhaps make a first, rather tentative distinction. Some models are tangible, symbolic representations of tangible things seen or yet to be seen. Some models are tangible symbolic representations of what is not tangible, and will not be until we give it form of some sort. In the former we can check for similarity in traits and functions. In the latter, we cannot. Here we have arbitrarily and deliberately made a metaphoric connection, and only persuasion makes it acceptable. The question of similarity cannot arise because we cannot check the tangible against the intangible. So maybe we can at least distinguish two types of disciplines. One group is concerned to give a new, clearer, more comprehensible form to what already has a form, but with greater complexity and less availability to perception. The model is designed to provide such perceptions.

Another group of disciplines is concerned to invent a form for what actually has no form: "group behavior," "choice," "motivation," "panic," "ambition," "devotion," and such. We give form in models to states of mind, to feelings, to ideas about thinking. You can see why it is that these kinds of quests for explanation are ultimately driven to seeking a material basis for the nonmaterial states. For so long as they remain "unembodied," we are always in danger either of taking metaphors too seriously or of dealing only with some supposed mythic powers. It is for this reason that the social sciences constantly make efforts to find tangible bases for tangible actions. We must, many social scientists believe, eliminate concepts such as "dignity," pride," "self-worth," even with concepts such as "mind," and attempt to replace them with some physical event. "Mind" must then become "brain." "Self-confidence" or "self-worth" must be reduced to levels of biochemical activity in the cerebrum. Even "pride" becomes the efficient recall of rewarded achievements in past testing encounters.

We have, thus, two distinct kinds of models. One seeks to explain and describe in tangible form what is already tangible, but needs both clearer, more precise description and explanation. The other seeks to describe and explain what is not tangible -- and it does so by inventing tangible forms in order to do so.

There is a third type of model whose purpose it is to give tangible form to feelings and thoughts, not to explain them, but to make them apparent to oneself and to others. It is a set of disciplines of a somewhat different order, with rather different purposes. Our immediate concern is with such questions as "communion," "community," "emotional support," "the need for intimacy," "orderly social relationships," and such. In these, we give body and form only by means of illustrative metaphors which always present us with the danger of taking the metaphors as literal disclosure. In this way, as we have shown earlier, concepts, feelings, hypotheses are not only made observable in things, they are in danger of becoming or being perceived as those things of which the model is made. And as *things* they can more securely be measured, weighed and tested. Nevertheless, if we remember to distinguish between a model and what it is we are modelling, then the social sciences are not natural sciences, exasperating as this may sound. Some social scientists fear the scandal of always having to deal with what is intangible. If that must be the case, how do we know that we have not modelled ghosts, goblins, and figments of some wild imagination? Well, we do not know, but what else can we do?

It brings up, again, the question on the nature of hypothesis. How do we distinguish, if indeed we can or ought to, between hypotheses in the natural sciences and those in the social sciences? Perhaps in this way: when we are dealing with the tangible matters of the world and their behaviors, a hypothesis is a statement of a logical connection between what can immediately be seen and what cannot yet be seen but which will appear at a later phase of some present event or function. In the social sciences, a hypothesis is not always a logical prediction of a future tangible event. It is rather an explanation of an intangible, given metaphoric form. And also an explanation of the metaphor itself.

Thus, it is a hypothesis that the movement of light is best understood in terms of and in the form of the movement of water. (Remember the ripple tank of your physics class?) The hypothesis is tested by the descriptions and behaviors of light in these terms, and by the supported explanations which later observations and experiments on the movement of light and water produce.

It is also a hypothesis to say that "oppression of a people ultimately produces revolution." To show what this means, we build a glass chamber and a movable pressure cap. When the cap is pressed down suddenly, the glass container will become increasingly brittle and explode. This, then, is what is meant by the statement, "oppression ultimately produces revolution or the breaking of the containing order." I suspect that most, if not all, social laws have this character. Now what, in terms of models and metaphors, can we say about this concept?

First and probably foremost, what do we say about the metaphoric implication that society is a glass container or that the rules of order in which a society lives, taken all together, is a glass container? Ridiculous! There is not the slightest point of similarity between social rules and glass containers.

But of course, no one intends or means to suggest an equivalence here. What is being suggested is that if you want to understand why societies "burst apart," just think of a glass container filled with something that needs the freedom to exchange energies with the air outside of the container. When pressure is applied, the inside must seek an outlet. When all outlets are sealed up, the container will crack simply by the pressures built within. No literal statement is involved or intended. The hypothesis here is an explanation of the metaphor itself. If it is accepted, some understanding accompanies the acceptance. But what we are called upon to do is establish some logical and empirical connection among elements of the model (the glass container, the sealing, the temper of glass, the pressure cover) and the concept under consideration. But this latter, now, takes on the form given to it by the model which at best is arbitrary. Someone could easily decide that such a model has no validity, no heuristic powers, for matters are confused when we treat societies as inert masses, contained with glass columns, with no alternatives. Besides, rules of society do not have the structure or the lack of resilience of a hollow glass column. Our skeptic might suggest a preference for a rubberized container which expands and contracts as pressure increases and decreases. This is much nearer to, it can be suggested, or closer to societal behavior than the former, glass model. Is it? Can any form of physical (observable) experiment validate the claim of "nearer to" or "closer to" for such matters? Not even the most detailed of statistical reports, either of what people say about oppression and their own resilience, or reports of what people have done in conditions of oppression, will confirm or refute the validity of such a model. For the simple fact is that "oppression" is not a tangible event like air, glass, and pressure caps. "Oppression" is a general term, defined differently in different contexts. And "pressure cap" here is a metaphor, not for a specific thing or action, but a form of catechresis, where we give to some event that has no name of its own, the name and form of something else which we have determined it is similar to.

Now, such problems as these are what sociologists, psychologists, philosophers, anthropologists, and economists are always facing. Physicists, chemists, meteorologists, and biologists do not have these problems. And it is this that distinguishes the hard sciences from the social sciences. When these social sciences borrow models from the natural sciences, and employ them as literally as it is possible, do the social sciences become natural sciences? I think not. I think they simply make the serious error of reducing metaphors to literal statements. The intangibles remain intangible despite the insistence to the contrary. For there is no possible way to prove that oppression is the pressure cap of a glass or rubber column. And the natural sciences, on the other hand, live or die by the proofs they provide for the claims they make.

Let me recap some points just made. Metaphors are used by all disciplines to make sense of the events that are the concern of each discipline. Whether those events are tangible, intangible or a mixture of both does not diminish the fact that metaphors are employed to analogize from something already known to something that is wished to be known. To invent that knowledge, metaphors can be cast in terms of tentative hypotheses that offer temporary suggestions of cognitive relationships between and among the events under scrutiny. To add to all of this, models are the tangible tools or instruments from which we attempt to explore the hypotheses suggested from our chosen metaphors.

When we remember that the world we live in contains tangible and intangibles, and that both require descriptions and explanations, it is wise to remember that some of our models are concerned with the tangible and some with the intangible; and we run serious risks of confusion when we discount the difference. But if we keep this in mind, we will be alert to what each model type does in each area of study, and what *kind* of claim it is making, and how it is to be treated. The natural sciences are never any more precise than are the social sciences, but for very different reasons. The one, because nature itself is always more than any model of it, always to be viewed increasingly microscopically or, conversely, on a grander, cosmic scene. The other is not precise because metaphor itself is never precise, especially when it deals with ideas that always change definition.

A word, and only a word, about mathematics. Here we have a discipline that is nothing but a set of rules for the manipulation of symbols without actual referents. Each symbol becomes, in essence, its own event. The symbol is given its meaning, and the meaning is constant, as are the rules for their transactions. Thus, mathematics is precise because it has neither tangible or nor intangible referents. What is developed, then, in mathematics are systems for quantifying the tangible and the intangible, but only because it has a referential world that transcends both the natural and the social worlds. That is what Bertrand Russell meant when he defined mathematics as a matter in which no one knows what he is talking *about*.

So we have a recommendation for distinguishing between the two forms of science which takes into account the arguments about the determinate roles of matter, and the supposed differences in methods, as well as the claim that distinguishing among the disciplines makes only for arbitrariness and confusion in our efforts to understand a seamless or seemless world.

Now, how about the third cluster of disciplines which we call the arts? How do we identify them? What do we study when we study any that are included here? Poetry, music, drama, dancing, painting, architecture, sculpture: the seven lively arts as they are called. I have already said what constitutes the primary differences, but more is required. The world in which we live, the world at hand, provides us with all the matters and concepts one needs to make life possible. For this we need even more precise descriptions of things and clarifications of meanings of statements made about the tangible and the intangible aspects of the world. But the world is not totally encompassed by explanations. However critical is the need to understand the ways of things and the meanings of the language we use about things and about ideas, we just as deeply appear to have a need for giving form to the feelings that we have about these two dimensions of our world. The models and metaphors that comprise any of the arts, then, do not have the function of explaining anything. They have, rather, the function of giving substance to our responses to things and ideas, of giving expression to feelings, to the sense of things, in their sensational qualities.

Much closer to the arbitrary nature of mathematics than to the natural sciences, and close enough to that aspect of the social sciences in the matter of giving form to intangibles, the arts yet differ from all of these in the invention of symbols and metaphors to be the embodiment of an aspect of life that neither physics, sociology nor mathematics is attentive to. Thus, when the poet, Archibald MacLeish, says that poems do not *mean*, they just are, we have a clue to what distinguishes the arts from all other disciplines. My feelings become the poem, the drama, the musical composition, the sculpture that I have produced. They have no other identity. I might go even further to say that if I do not give them some tangible form, in words, colors, lines, musical notes or dance movements, how can I persuade you to believe that they even exist or have being? And if I give them no embodiment, does it mean I have no feelings? No. It means I have feelings that have no form, and therefore which you cannot perceive or understand. One vast dimension of life lies forever unformed, unpresented, unapproached, and unapproachable. A person without art, then, is a grubby thing, whose sensitivities to the qualities and textures and colors of the world lay beyond concern or consideration. To dismiss these responses as being merely subjective, merely personal is to demean an entire range of human activities by the prevention of the expression of a complete realm of feelings.

And yet, what is psychology but the construction of models and metaphors for purposes of explaining feelings? Perhaps works of art ought to be part of the subject matter that psychology addresses. Well, it does. It attempts to explain, first, what the feelings mean in a context of feelings and relationships of one person to other people and things. Then it explains why this particular form in the work is chosen to symbolize this particular feeling, and what else is signified by such a choice. But it must be said that however complete such a description and explanation of a work are, it does not encompass that other domain, the domain that embodies feelings without the need to explain them. In fact, in modern criticism of any work in art, the psychological models of explanation have so taken over, even in the ordinary conversation of common sense people, that the aspect of art as expression of being comes more and more to be lost or trivialized. And with it, the world of celebration and bacchanal; the force of tragedy and laughter are dismissed as only personal disgorgings of frustration or mindless elation. Small wonder that artists often feel themselves aliens in the business of the world, and then compensate for it by defining themselves as an elite, concerned with only truly important things of life and of humanity. In our terms, they are neither outside the pale of the business of the world, nor are they an elite endowed with mysterious powers of revelation of the great wonders of the world.[2] They are the givers of new perceptions of the textures, the colors, the sounds, and forms of the work seen as events in their own qualities. But in an important respect, they are no different from the scientists, the anthropologists, the historians, or mathematicians, who also give us new perceptions, but of other dimensions of the world in which we live.

The poet tells us and enables us to perceive what it is to "push hard against the sea." The oceanographer allows us to perceive the power and the effects and conditions of water pressure. The two perceptions are very different, and are not suitable substitutes for each other. You cannot read one statement and understand the other, or confuse one for the other. But together, the sense and the meaning of the sea presents us with a richer understanding of what is, and our perceptions of it.

2

The same thing can be said of scientists who delve into the wonderful secrets of the universe. Many people say, almost with an ironic pride, that they could not comprehend what physicists talk about and are grateful!

But does one learn to be an artist in the sense that one learns to be a physicist or a sociologist or a philosopher? This is usually asked in a scornful way -- implying that you are either born with talent, with genius, or you will never be an artist. (This is often believed not only by people who are not artists but by artists too!) My answer is, at least, Heaven help us all if it is not possible to learn to invent models and metaphors of expression, just as we can obviously learn to invent models and metaphors for explanation! Neither task is easy, of course. But one is as possible as the other, and each is matured in the constant practice of such inventions. After all, that is precisely what this whole book is all about.

Nor is art any more a matter of intuition, divine guidance, or sudden flashes of unaccountable visions than is hypotheses construction. There is a logic of invention in both cases, however appealing the notion of "inborn" powers may be.

The "Un-Naturalness" of the Disciplines

Let me recapitulate the basic ideas of this chapter, if for no other reason than in the interest of orderliness.

The basic question was that of distinguishing the various disciplines from one another for distinctively educational purposes. The problem was: how does one learn to think, not generally, but quite specifically in each of the subjects or disciplines that constitute a school curriculum or program? Why such distinctions? Why so many disciplines? What of the argument that these distinctions are only for administrative purposes? Meaning that some administrator arbitrarily invented them for his/her own purposes of comfort and control. I suggested that this view did not take into account the logic of the division of a complex world into more manageable segments, in the interests of greater understanding of what the world is and what potentials reside within it. Nor does it take into account the educational activity of becoming skilled in the use of the models each discipline has created for exploring some domain or aspect of that enormously complex thing we call life. We return to the view that the world of nature does not organize itself. It does not give itself names and classifications. Disciplines, as they are born and develop, do for nature what nature cannot do for itself: transmit to each new member of each new generation the models and metaphors that make perception of the world possible. It is these models and metaphors that give the world the character and distinctions and the order that we have inherited from previous generations and which we now see in it. So if our minds did not create the physical world, then our thinking is the activity that has given that world order, meaning, features, and potentials for use.

Each discipline, I have argued, is concerned with its own facet of that world, some with its physical features and functions, some with the modes of thinking about such things, and some with the expressions of human feelings about all that is experienced. Together, they comprise all the possibilities of reflection and action that constitute a human environment. It is a fact that each discipline is a model-making, a metaphor-inventing and using activity. An activity that enables us in turn to learn to think in ways which identify each of these modes of exploring, explaining, and expressing our feelings and thoughts about the world. And, even more importantly, those models and metaphors that give us, at the outset, our perceptions of the world. Thereafter, the act of thinking is an act of altering and re-creating those very models and metaphors, and thereby altering them and our very perceptions of the world we inhabit.

7.

METAPHORS, MODELS

AND THE DISCIPLINES

If you have journeyed with me to this stage of this work, you will have already formulated some basic concepts that distinguish the various disciplines. Moreover, you will have already exercised your curiosity to examine again that poem from English literature class or that physics model discussed, or even spent some time looking for the models and metaphors embedded in that chapter on economics that you recently read. You will have found, hopefully, much to your delight, that once trained in finding and determining the models and metaphors in a work, you can derive not only a deeper, richer appreciation of the role of thinking in the creation of the disciplines, but a richer understanding of the models of those disciplines.

We return to something that was promised to you in the first chapter. Your experiences at the college level will provide you with many new views of "how the world goes." Your answer now, if you have subscribed to my thesis, is "it goes by metaphor." The necessary and sufficient conditions that characterizes the action of thinking is metaphor-making and metaphor-using. At some other time during your life, you might reject this whole thesis and substitute another: thus is the nature of our being. But for now, however temporary, you can commend yourself for learning the basic principles that have guided this work and you now have a greater understanding of "how the world goes." No longer will the courses and disciplines you learn be disjunctive, seemingly unconnected and without common foundation. You may also shed some of those old conceptual shackles that have limited and stunted your thinking. You natural science majors may even find beauty, rhythm, and color in the arts; you artists may find a new appreciation of the sciences; and the psychologists and philosophers among you may find new energies and devotion to your chosen field. And one more thing: it should have created greater thirst for more information on the distinction among the disciplines. This is what this chapter is concerned with. In it, I have tried to expand on each of the disciplines, and for the sake of comparison, juxtaposed them against one another to further clarify the purpose and intent of each relative to the major concepts developed in the previous six chapters. In an earlier work (Belth, 1977), I expanded more fully on the distinction among these major categories of disciplines, and I would encourage examination of that work to enhance your understanding and further support for what I have said here.

The Arts

If you asked a group of artists about the models of the world that they are creating, they might answer, "We don't know what you're talking about. We only use live models." Or they might say, "We never theorize about our work. We only do it. You want theory, go to the philosophers or the critics who don't know anything about art anyway. Art is a skill, a technique. You don't need theory for that. The people who theorize or write criticism are people who don't have the talent to be artists anyway."

And if you should ask (Heaven forbid!) what the work is a metaphor for or a metaphor of, the artist could yell, "You've been reading that Belth stuff again. Get the hell outta here. I don't use metaphor or make them. That kind of stuff just kills good art." Try to argue, and the artist will have the upper hand every time. You only just talk. Even if you make a remarkably astute and flattering comment, the response most likely will be, "Oh yeah? I wasn't thinking about that at all. But if you say it's there, that's okay with me. I don't explain what I am doing. I just do it." So you ask, "But why did Robert Delaunay paint the Eiffel Tower as a dancer? The metal legs, thrust out in a dancer's position?" "Who knows?" you will be told. "That's the way he sees the Tower. It's happy, even though it is steel, and it makes you joyful when you look at his painting. So he paints it as a dancer. That's pretty obvious, isn't it? I just don't see it that way, so I don't paint it that way. I see it as a tall, rigid monument to engineering, so I paint it *that* way. What further information can I give you?"

What, indeed? Now, all this is not meant as a warning to avoid talking with artists, you understand. What I am suggesting is that while looking at a painting, if you have to talk to the artist, listen very carefully to what is said. The artist may in fact state the very thing that he insisted no attention is paid to whatsoever.

Take the sentence, "That is the way he sees the Tower." You many accuse me of having put that down just to play tricks on the artist, to make him say what I want him to say in order to prove some point of mine. Except for one thing: the statement is so simple, so direct, and so exactly what a painter had, in fact, said. And the latter sentence, "I just don't see it that way. I see it as ...." That too, is a direct quote, and the kind of statement any artist is likely to make and has made again and again.

What this corroborates, I believe, is my argument that in some fields of endeavor the making of metaphors, the creation of new models of the world, are not necessarily conscious acts, nor do they have to be. But consciousness does not enhance the act, nor does absence of consciousness detract or diminish the originality of the act. A concern for the level of awareness or consciousness of the basis on which the quality or the significance of the thing created is of concern to the analyst or theoretician of aesthetics, not to the artist at work. An artist may tell you, if insightful enough, that every work of art is a metaphor, providing the observer with a new model of some aspect of reality. The artist's attention is elsewhere, as it must be. Work must be done, a skill must be managed, materials need to be gathered and presented, images evoked, sounds formed, balances created between word sounds and imagery if the art is to do what is intended: the projection of one's feelings about the world.

But our artist might pause and tell you, "Don't you see how background and foreground meet at this line, each to give the other a contrast in form through line and color? Look over there. Don't you see how the line creates a form in nature? See how all the other things (trees, houses, hills) make a whole in their balance of line and color? That's what I've done here. Look at the painting, and see if you don't see the landscape that way."

While the artist might deny that through the painting you are given "new eyes" with which to see the world, but isn't that just what is being done? What the painter has done is alter emphases, colors, lights, relationships of some actual landscape in order to make the painter's sight of the things your sight of those same things.

Perhaps a duller example can illustrate this point. Have you ever bought something, say a bicycle, that came in parts and which you had to put together? All the parts come with a set of instructions that gives you "exploded" diagrams of the various parts, which piece goes with which, how they are attached, what sequence to follow in putting it together. The picture of what it will actually look like when it is properly done is accurate, but not exactly what the bicycle looks like. There are labels, arrows, and insert drawings added. The instructions enable you to see the bicycle in a somewhat different way than it is seen when completely put together. But the instruction sheets have given you a new or added perception of the bike.

Now, few paintings are depictions of the skeleton of something, and none explicitly tell you what to put with what in order to see what is represented in the painting -- a landscape, a seascape, a human face or figure, a field of hay, whatever. And yet, metaphorically speaking, isn't this what a work of art really does? Does it not direct you to see the world as the artist has seen it? And if a work of art does not do this, then what in the world does it do? The artist makes a model of the world, but one that can be comprehended and enjoyed in a different way as perhaps nature itself cannot.

Take the artist and the created model. In looking at a portrait, we eagerly look for the likeness between the painting and the person who modeled it. But surely the work is more than just a matter of likeness. Surely the painting presents more than similarity between it and the person. Colors that may not be precisely the colors of the face, body, clothing, eyes, present us with more than just mirror-perfect reflections. The posture has import. The new colors are suggestive of more than the surface of the real person or thing. A balance in relationship between forms of persons and objects. What the artist observes as a special or unique quality in the face, gaze, or posture is brought into a focus that is perhaps not present in the actuality. The portrait is suddenly more than a picture: it is a perception. The model used has now become a model of perception created in and embodied in the portrait. If likeness is not immediately apparent to us and we are first thrown off because of this, little by little we find ourselves seeing, not the portrait as a person, but the person in the portrait.

Picasso once painted a portrait of Gertrude Stein. She looked at it, unhappily, and said, "That's not me." He answered, "Don't worry. You will look like that after awhile." Now what do most of us know about Gertrude Stein's appearance? Not what photographs tell us, but what Picasso's portrait makes us see. It is not the model who becomes the painting: it is the painting that becomes a model or perception of something in the world. But we do not recognize this immediately. For the most part, we look at paintings of the world, but separate the two. We may marvel at the technique of the artist, the use of the brush, the colors used, the forms presented, and we enjoy the work as it stands. Unwittingly, thereafter, nature takes the form of the painting, and suddenly, the vision in the painting is the vision we have of the world. We may take a drive through the countryside and find ourselves "seeing" Van Gogh's earth shapes or Renoir's lush foliage, or Monet's poppy fields. But the world is not the model for these paintings. The model becomes the world we see afterwards.

What I have said so far about the arts has dealt primarily with painting. What then of poetry? A couple of things need to be reviewed at this point. The first is that of explanation. Like painting, poetry offers no explanation of the world. Its intention is not to offer why the poet believes such and such, for it does not intend to provide for the reader a reason for seeing the world that way. The purpose of poetry is rather to celebrate inner worlds of feelings and emotions that have been re-presented in the language of the poem. Does this mean that poetry, along with all the other arts, is less of a discipline, than say, history or the natural sciences? If you have been following my arguments thus far, you should anticipate that my answer will have to be an emphatic *"NO!"* If the sciences stand in testimony to our efforts to understand the external world in all its complexities, in all its intricacies, then the poetry stands in testimony to the exploration of one's own "inner world," by which feelings, emotions, desires, terrors, are all given meaning through our language, however limited that language might be. To require that the poet explain the metaphors used, to demand more than what the poet has written in the expression of him or herself, shifts the intent of poetry from that celebration of feelings and emotions to consider why the poet feels that way. No longer is the product of the poet's mind a celebration, but a way of understanding of how the poet thinks, and therefore in the realm of psychology.

Perhaps in no other area of thinking is the playful quality of thinking so manifest as it is in the area of poetry. For here, unlike the sciences or history, the poet is allowed to conjure up any image that seems appropriate to represent the feelings depicted. And this is precisely because the poet deals with language, rather than any observable event or thing. This being the case, the poet deals with the softest of models, since the referents depicted in the poem are not the words themselves, but those "inner states," those feelings, desires, and emotions that the poem is attempting to conceptualize. So the poet need not explain feelings and emotions, only depict them in the form of a poem. In order to do that, the poet employs the playful use of words, bringing together unusual and interesting combinations of concepts to represent what is intangible. Thus, "stones that speak" (pathetic fallacy) or "the darkest light" (oxymoron) are created to produce illusions that no other area of thinking can. For when we speak of the "darkest light," we readily understand that the poet is not speaking literally, since you would dismiss such a combination of words as absurd. When understood that the poet is not talking about light at all, but rather some feeling, for instance, a last glimmer of hope in a desperate situation, then we can see how the metaphor gives us a new vision, a new image that literal statements simply cannot.

History

Think for a moment about history and historical writing. There appears to be prevalent the view that history is a portrait of a period, a series of events, a person, a conflict, a development. And, of course, one could certainly justify such a view. We can surely say that a good history is a detailed portrait, in words, of the "face and form" of some selected period of the past.

But some special qualifications must be made that emphasize the metaphoric use of the term "portrait." The word ordinarily refers to a painting, but can of course be used more broadly, provided it is used to point to what is generally identified as a portrait. Some likeness ought to be present, but as I have just pointed out, the likeness in a portrait does not need to be a "picture" of the person. It might be a "likeness" of a quality, of a general form, of features seen in a special perspective. However, and here is an important point, in the portrait which is a painting, the subject is present, either actually or in some replica, say a photograph or a sketch made earlier. In historical "portraits," however, an event or a whole series of events is the subject that are no longer present for the historian. Yes, there may be and invariably are records, other written "portraits," documents, artifacts that are available for use by the historian. But the historian can no more mirror the events of the past than the artist can mirror the subject that is painted. In similar ways, the historian must re-form the matters, the events of the past, emphasizing some features and behaviors while de-emphasizing others. Some things are added and some things are deleted. During this task, some lives are given focus while others are diluted with the purpose of showing connections, accumulations, dissolutions, that the documents and the artifacts might imply. These implications are read out by the historian who seeks to demonstrate that they are reasonable, logical, and justifiable by other events in the portrait of time. It is good history when there is coherence in the portrait, when the presence of some features explain and lead us to anticipate the appearance or the presence of others; when from the portrait we derive a sense of wholeness, or why the sense of wholeness has been broken or scattered.

What emerges from history, so understood, is more than a record of "how it really was," but a model of the time, the people, the events, which we can examine again and again, and use in an effort to understand the actualities that form the subject matter of that work.

Admittedly, this is all very general, and thus perhaps too abstract. What I am saying is that neither the artist nor the historian, in thinking and doing, is totally or even partially determined by the materials confronted as the subject matter. Each brings to the work concepts, specific visions, sets of feelings and thoughts, which become the true subject matter of the work.   The portrait of Gertrude Stein has, as its subject matter, not the face and figure of that lady, but the perceptions of the painter.   A portrait of the beginnings of the United States does not have the data of that extended period as its subject matter, but a historian's perceptions, employed to organize that collection or aggregate of data.

But, as in a portrait, the question of "How was it, *really*?" is an interesting directive. The very nature of the question suggests that the historian should step away from the work and avoid intruding on the data in order to report only what the data reveals is a curious one.   It bespeaks the view that events must be allowed to speak for themselves, free from the coloring predispositions of historians, or the temptation they have to see in the past only what they want to see. But the alternative question would have to be: Can the historian do this? Is it possible, after reading some data, to do other than read into that data the structures of the historian's own knowledge and mental constructs?   In other words, can either the artist or the historian dispense with their own minds and then go on to paint a portrait of a person or write a portrait of an age?   How could such a work be done? Even a computer, designed to record precisely what is received, operates only on a previously prepared program placed into it. That program takes the incoming data or records and sorts, organizes, and interprets. So even to be as "neutral" as a computer is not to be very neutral at all. Do away with the program and you do away with the computer as a functioning instrument. What remains is just a bunch of hardware.   Do away with the perceptual and conceptual instruments of the historian and all you have is a creature with receptors with no means of organizing, explaining, or interpreting what is received. What then would history be? Curiously, is anyone free to explain and interpret except the historian?   Surely that could not be what is intended. Probably what is being said is that the events recorded carry their own meanings and their own messages.   The historian, by following precisely the logic of events, will set forth only what is precisely implied.   And this returns us to an earlier question: does the data of nature or the data of the past have a voice of its own? Is it best understood only if we listen, neutrally, unencumbered by our own anticipations and our own sorting systems?   Carry this discussion to some kind of completion on your own.   I want to talk about another problem that is hinted here.

In terms of "portraits" and the suggested analogy, are we then to consider history an art? If, as I have argued, one does not write history as a simple chronicle of events in their proper sequence with proper accuracy, but if the historian does what the painter does, is there nothing left to distinguish art from history? I do not want to make mountains about the obvious, as the difference is not difficult to find.

In painting, in fact in all art, the imagery that is created, even from the most solid parts of the world, need not answer to the world in any way. The logic of art is quite a different order than the logic of science or of history. In art, the logic is a matter of the projected internal relationships between imagined or imaginary events. It is possible to create a work of art in which all men walk about on one finger, in which angels and cherubs play golf, in which princesses pursue and capture unicorns, in which a pope can be captain of a baseball team. Whatever nature or society may say about the illogic of such works, neither the work of art nor the artist is obliged to respond. The logic lies between the symbols, without reference to the "way the world really is." It is a logic of the relation of symbols to symbols -- of the symbol of helpless purity (the unicorn) and lonely aggressiveness (the princess). It is not the logic of actuality, but of imagined worlds.

This would suggest to you one of the major differences between art and history. For where the artist is not limited to or by reality, the historian serves the evidence encountered. Lacking this evidence, there are assertions that cannot be made. When invention is free, coming out of imagination alone, the work loses its claim as history, as historical scholarship. To interpret, to reconstruct, to give new meaning is one thing. But to reconstruct from no evidence, if that is possible, is not to write history, but to write fairy tales or myths. Writing a history of Germany from 1932 to 1945, and all the time insisting that death camps did not exist, is to cease doing history and becoming instead a publicist for some special, private cause.

The other distinction I have made much of already. This is the difference in intention. Art, I have shown, is not intended to explain a world, only to re-present it as perceived by the artist, bearing its import as feeling. But if history does not explain, what does it do? It is this matter of providing explanation which not only distinguishes history from art, but history from mere chronicle.

Following these two differences between art and history, we might look for a moment at the metaphors intrinsic, so to speak, to history and to art, as well as to the models constructed and used in each. It must be appreciated, for what has been said, that aesthetic metaphors, metaphors of expression, will be metaphors that provide for the absurd, for humor and comedy, for fantastic worlds. Primarily, then, these would be in the form of pathetic fallacy. For in the arts, dogs, trees, fire-hydrants and skull bones speak, sing or row boats. Leaves may take the forms of faces, Eiffel Towers may dance, whales swallow people and cough them up again with great distaste.

But try this as you are trying to write history and you have moved to writing stories only. It is possible to commit one's efforts to the uses of synecdoche, but not for long, lest history be reduced to portraying a time, an age in the terms of a single feature. Such a reduction of the complexities of a person or an age would show the thin lines of caricature, and be limited to that extent in its explanatory power. The arts, on the whole, are better constituted, by purpose and method, to the uses of synecdoche, for the exaggeration of a feature and reduction of evidence is not required to answer to the world of data and of facts.

It would appear that history, because of its obligations to attend to evidence and because of the nature of that evidence (that is always a record of the past), must rely heavily on analogy. For it is only by means of analogy that we can address a past that does not return, that cannot be repeated in what might have been its original character and sequence. Now, although this will weaken any claim that history may make to being a science, it does strengthen the argument that it is not one of the arts. Nevertheless, how else does one see the past, partake of its pulses and its tensions, its disputes and its passions, its prides and its humiliation, except by means of analogy?

And after an analogy has been worked out, tested and become accepted as leading to a genuine understanding of evidence, the even truer test comes in the development of some metonymies. For only by altering sequences, causes and effects, seeing wholes of a different character as individual events, does the analogy receive a fuller evaluation. A richer understanding and explanation of any historical portrait is achieved when alternatives in cause and sequence, of primariness and secondariness are offered and used to test a first explanation. We know more about the beginnings of America's involvement in World War II when we take seriously the possibility that the report of its beginnings given out by President Roosevelt may have provided us with a sequence of events that can be turned around, and better read backwards. The historian who does not use this device may be too easily pleased by the persuasive character of a chosen analogy, too delighted by the "story" it allows to be told. And when oxymoron would appear, the effects in the history would not so much be illuminated by sharp contrasts as a flowery ornamentation that can only be distracting, not explanatory.

So historical thinking, which manifests itself in the writing of history, is not truly an art, despite its occasional similarities in its metaphoric operations. It must keep itself anchored to whatever evidence of actual events it has available. In modern times, with the marvelous instruments of recording, record-keeping, record-testing, and analyzing, it would seem to be much easier to do this than it was just a short time ago, and as it still is when the concern is to explore and explain events long ago. But that may not be altogether so. Along with the prevalence of records, there has grown up an awareness of the complexities of psychological states of mind, of political tactics, of new forms of interpretation, that does not allow even the seemingly fullest record of evidence to "speak for itself." Besides, the fuller "historical" effects of any event cannot be examined until time itself has been given for such effects to develop. Take the events that involved Richard Nixon. The singular question that keeps arising is, "Why did he do the things that he did?" Well, psychologists seem best equipped to answer such a question. But can history be reduced to psychology? If it can, then what happens to history? Is history merely the record of human motives? Or is it, rather, what changes over a period of time occur by such and such actions? To explain why the actions were taken does not even touch the widening or narrowing consequences of those actions, whatever the psychological causes or determinations. When people say that historians will have to wait before they can evaluate and explain an event, it is not always because more evidence is needed to understand its causes, but rather that more time is needed to observe the consequences of the action. What they are waiting for then is the consequences to develop. And, in the case of ex-President Nixon, they have developed only to a small degree in the short period of time since his resignation.

Perhaps all this suggests that history is really a science, or potentially a science. For a concern with what actually happened and what is happening, the measuring of behavioral outcomes seems to be what science is all about. If the best of history is the explanation of behaviors and changes when the intrusions of the explorer are kept to a minimum, isn't that akin to what the natural scientists are most careful of? Aren't both history and science concerned to produce bodies of knowledge that continued investigation will either corroborate or demonstrate to be wrought with error? To be sure. But, before we draw such a conclusion, we should perhaps consider more carefully what science is, what scientists do, and how they do it; in short, what scientific thinking is.

The Natural Sciences

The insistence that science is a body of proven, tested and testable knowledge is a statement only about its claims and conclusions. It is not a statement about its processes and what elements are part of those processes. For one thing, in the *bodies of knowledge* statement, no distinction is made between the study of some event and the inference that that event belongs to some class. Testing a drop of water, for example, is testing a sample of *all* water; testing for the frequency and wavelength of this beam of light is testing for the structure of *all* light.

But historically exploring the basis of decisions of Louis XIV is not testing for the basis of decisions of all the Louis, from I through XVIII, or for all royalty, wherever they may be found, in whatever time. If this were so and some valid claims could be reached, resulting in the creation of a body of knowledge, then again we are not involved in history, but in psychology or biology. But the body of knowledge that historians make available to us has a different character than those which the physicist, the biologist or the psychologist presents to us. Where science sums up for us the behaviors and the structures of individual things as representing the behavior of all such things within a given class, history is not obligated to do the same.

The body of knowledge that the historian gives us is always particular of individuals, whose actions and decisions have affected the lives of other individuals, not as members of a class of all such individuals, but who happen to be members of this or that social group.

From science we can make generalizations as can be determined to be laws of behavior or explanatory laws. But this presupposes that there will be and are conditions that affect all members of the same class in exactly the same way. Adhering, for instance, to the "laws" of natural selection for the evolution of finches of the Galapagos Islands, but not the evolution of an opposing thumb in humans, seems to us, well, unscientific. We assume or presuppose that the same process or mechanism that has given the finches so many different types of beaks should be the same process or mechanism that has given humans their opposing thumbs. That is why a law can explain. Can we write the same kinds of laws of history? I must tell you that there are historians who not only believe it can be done, and that it is the responsibility of the historians to do just that, but who actually do or try to do so. And if they can, then history is indeed a science.

Which raises for us two interesting questions. When we write a law of history, what does it refer to? And what, considering the usual focus of the historian's concern, is now eliminated so that such a law can be written? Moreover, if the concern of science is to write laws of behavior and of explanation, what happens to the earlier definition that science is a body of proven knowledge? Does one contradict the other? Sustain the other? Or are they saying something entirely different, each of them, which has no effect on the other? In terms of what I have said above, I would be tempted to conclude that they are saying entirely different things which may have no relation to one another, but which would appear to make the body of knowledge concept an insignificant one. If we keep the two separate, this is what it comes to. One is a statement about claims or conclusions, the other about processes. But a body of knowledge can accumulate from any source whatever -- tradition, sudden insight, rough experience, mystical disclosures, or careful exploration and analysis among a peer group. All would have to be included. If, however, the process is the primary element or determinant of science, then only the last is the proper, reliable source from which a body of knowledge is derived. How would this affect the writing of history? Significantly, I suspect. Too much of randomness of human behavior enters into the matters which are the subject of history, and too much which can never be tested a second time by a group of peer scholars.

One further example to illustrate this difference between history and science. Not so long ago, it was reported that nuclear fusion had been achieved in the laboratory at normal temperatures. This was heralded by the press and, unfortunately, by some scientists also, as a major breakthrough in the use of nuclear fusion as an energy source. Attempts to replicate the process, however, led to extremely disappointing results as no other group could duplicate the same reaction. The attempt to make it happen again, using the same procedures, demonstrates the hallmark of science -- that science requires the ability to duplicate results. The same luxury is not afforded to history. The historian cannot go back to the assassination of John F. Kennedy and *re-do* it to find causes and human motives. The historian relies only on the records, no matter how scant or extensive, left after the event.

We need to examine another presupposition of science to see how its character has shaped what can be called classical science, but when finally rejected, led the way to the more modern approaches to science.

At an earlier time, probably under the influence of theology and religious beliefs, it was believed that the universe was orderly and harmonious, either by its very nature or by divine design. On this basis, science was the quest for the discovery of that orderliness, and an effort to describe it as precisely as possible. Nothing more. Today's science has given up this presupposition to a great extent. It has come to entertain the view that perhaps nature, the whole universe, is rather a random thing. That, if there is a logic in nature, it is the logic of internal relationships between things and things, things and forces, none of which is imposed upon nature by a divine logician or by nature seen to operate under external, logical rules. From such a new presupposition, science is concerned not simply to say what is, but to explain why things happen the way they do, when they do, even in a random universe. And that even in a random universe we can write laws that enable us to perceive some order. Thus, science moves from discovery to invention; from discovering what is to inventing models which, when applied, enable us to construct order where there is perhaps none. Once this presupposition is accepted and comes into play, the whole of what T.S. Kuhn has called "normal science" takes on a new character, becoming a wholly different process. The "logic of discovery" is either replaced by a "logic of invention" or the term "discover" comes to have an entirely new definition.   This shift of emphasis in scientific thinking produces a much different perspective on the purpose of science. While knowledge about the external world still is important, science is now characterized more specifically by the construction of models (Kuhn calls them "paradigms") of inquiry and explanation. Moreover, with the abdication of the assumption about an innate order to the universe, science can also be concerned with learning what would happen "if this were mixed with that," "this seen *as* that," "this transformed by that." In other words, what other potentials are there in the universe than those we now know? With this direction, physicists can spend billions of dollars on particle accelerators to smash atoms apart and to detect infinitesimally small particles that may or may not have a corresponding reality in nature.   What is important, however, is that our accumulating knowledge about such particles and their behaviors allow for the construction of models that will give us the "grand view" or "grand design" of the universe and matter.   So science has become, even more completely, a process of creating models, beyond those we normally use, from which entirely new laws of the behavior of things might be written. The world of *what is* must now be read as "the world of what else could be and how do we bring about things we do not yet know?"

An interesting, if not curious illustration of this other-than-ordinary view of science is a recent book published under the title, *Encyclopedia of Ignorance*.[1] Some twenty or thirty scientists were asked the question, not about the level of knowledge that their individual disciplines have reached, but rather from what is already known in your field, what are you ignorant of and what would you like to know? For a field of study that has so long identified itself as the reservoir of reliable knowledge to now identify itself as a field of ignorance is a startling change indeed.   Nor is this just a facetious or ironic game.   For what it really asks, I suggest, is: what do the prevailing models of inquiry prevent you from knowing, and what models do you think need to be constructed in order to banish that ignorance?   In one way or another, the essays in that volume address themselves to just that very question.

What develops from all this is a resurrection of an idea probably originated by Descartes in the 17th Century -- that science is primarily method. But it is no longer considered a method which quickly becomes *the* method.   It is now

---

[1]

Ronald Duncan and Miranda Smith (1979).

considered method-making, a process that cannot be reduced to something we cozily call the "scientific method." There may be rules we could distill, or propose for the construction of a model, from which some method could arise, but such rules are not drawn from some infallible source. They are human prescriptions, which other humans alter constantly. So the "scientific method" may be just a lingering vestige of Aristotle, Bacon, Descartes, Dewey or God. If creativity is God's domain, and we start creating new methods and models all over the place, then (Heaven help us!) we are now in God's domain, and can be talked about as God cannot.[2]

The construction of models, in and of itself, cannot be the distinguishing criterion since as disciplines, art, history, natural sciences, and the social sciences all construct models. You will remember that I have said that science attempts to construct models of inquiry and explanation, and so does history. But the purpose of science is to wonder about the possible new kinds of behaviors in observable matters thus far undetected or not considered important in the establishment of causal relationships. History, on the other hand, is also concerned with behaviors, but behaviors that have led to certain consequences in the course of human events.

Since science is concerned with the construction of models of inquiry and explanation, can this discipline be considered history? What distinguishes science from history that makes science one type of discipline and history another?
The construction of models, in and of itself, cannot be the distinguishing criterion since as disciplines, art, history, natural sciences and the social sciences all construct models. You will remember that I have said that science attempts to construct models of inquiry and explanation, and so does history. But the purpose of science is to wonder about the possible new kinds of behaviors in observable matters thus far undetected or not considered important in the establishment of causal relationships. History, on the other hand, is also concerned with behaviors, but behaviors that have led to certain consequences in the course of human events and which have affected later lives of individuals, groups or society.

Another difference, already mentioned, deals with the construction of general laws which recommend how things will behave and how events will unfold within a narrow perspective of exploring the world. These laws of nature are written

---

2

Can't you hear the howls of denunciation against vain pride, against committing the first deadly sin? And is science now, as some would have you believe, simply the new and terrifying theology?

with respect of events that exercise no voluntary choice for their behaviors. Rocks must fall when drawn by gravity; oak trees must produce oak seeds; the digestive system must function as enzymes are secreted and food is hydrolyzed. History has no such restriction. If there are laws of history, then they are only temporary, as humans make decisions which fly in the face of automatic tendencies, often in violation of them.

What kinds of metaphors does each depend upon to construct models? More often than not, the natural sciences depend on the invention of analogies so that something, not readily apparent to the senses, can be compared to something else which can be readily observed. Thus, we come to *see*, meaning we conceive, light behaving as water behaves, or atoms behaving as tiny solar systems. History, too, depends on analogy construction. In history, we explain, not the nature of things, but the reasons for this set of actions and changes in human development. By the use of analogy, we can see Adolph Hitler as a hysterical Napoleon. (Not very subtle, but you get the point.) What distinguishes the two disciplines in the use of analogies are the events about which each discipline creates analogies. The analogies of science are testable in direct observation. The analogies of history are testable only in a logical, psychological or literary sense; a very different kind of test, you will notice. Given this distinction, history seems much closer to the arts in terms of the kinds of analogies used than it is to the sciences, in spite of the fact that history and science are concerned with actualities, while the arts use the actual to create other than actualities.

One further point regarding the creation of analogies. By their very nature, analogies must always produce a large degree of tentativeness in their conclusions. This is why the sciences use analogy more sparingly than does history. In the latter, I have said, the only way we can reach back into time to understand change is by means of analogy. In the former, analogy is used primarily to deal with what cannot, for the moment, be seen. By and large, modern science admits that sometimes it deals with "matters" that may never be seen. It is argued that "quarks," what current science considers the fundamental particles of nature, are pure hypothetical constructs. Thus, the only way to talk about quarks and their behavior is through analogy. In history, consequences are as conjectural as the analogies themselves, and thus, the claims of history are as open to dispute as the analogies upon which that history is written.

The natural sciences are much more likely to use metonymy, for the sciences are always concerned with questions of "what if ...?" What if, instead of this sequence of events, another sequence is introduced? What if, instead of this as the cause, the effect can be considered the cause? What if the model can be turned around? What if one model is abandoned and another adopted?

But I have shown already that history, too, depends on the use of metonymy at some point in its thinking. We again encounter the same differences that existed in the use of analogy in both disciplines -- that of testability. In science, there is always the necessity of testing the referents of actuality. In history, on the other hand, the metonymies are purely verbal, making them open only to logical and linguistic analyses, not direct experimentation.

As with history, the use of pathetic fallacy in the sciences produces a claim for the existence of goblins, spirits, and ghosts in machines, rocks, water, foliage, with "minds of their own." From this we do not get science: we get science fiction.[3] If you want to argue that science often derives from science fiction, I would only suggest it does so only when fanciful hypotheses are transformed into metonymies of the actual. It is notable that the "Star Trek" series on television and six *Star Trek* movies have been a special favorite of scientists in the United States and probably elsewhere. Who can doubt it? Who would more enjoy the fictions of science than scientists themselves? Aside from any catharsis this and other science fiction would offer, who is more likely and better able to envision fantastic worlds arising from fantastic discoveries than those among us who engage in the invention of new powers and potentials in the actual world.

Natural science, too, more than any other discipline will employ catechresis. It is in science, after all, more than in any other pursuit that we must think about things without names, powers that have no identity, relative to the terms of things and powers we already know. To understand this function of science and the role that catechresis plays in it, makes possible newer and more promising, though unexpected, testing of both the known and, until now, unknown.

We have hardly done more than introduce the concept of scientific thinking, as we did no more than introduce aesthetic thinking and historical thinking. But we need to summarize the aspects of scientific thinking before we move on to the social sciences.

Scientific thinking is involved with the construction of models of inquiry and explanation about the natural events that occur in the world. Since the world, its objects and events, become the referents of these models, science must be involved with constructing very hard models. This is so that the knowledge constructed can be reliable, testable, and able to be duplicated by peers. Scientists, upon the invention of some model or metaphor to explain or inquire

---

[3] With one notable exception that has already been mentioned. The theory of natural selection is a fine example of pathetic fallacy in the natural sciences.

into some event, cannot turn around and state that no one should test for it. This would be an extreme violation of the fundamental presuppositions of the natural sciences. It is this qualification that separate the natural sciences from the other disciplines of the arts and history.

The Social Sciences

We must expect any analysis of the social sciences to be more complicated than the same treatment of the other types of disciplines. The obvious reason for this is that a number of apparently different disciplines fall under one classification. So the first question we will have to be answered is, do all of the social sciences share a common mode of thinking? Is that why they all fall within one classification? Is it that they share the same kind of data? Perhaps the term *social sciences* itself is misleading? Should we get rid of it, free these disciplines from the bond (or bondage?) or reclassify them into some other, prevailing and more familiar group?

I shall try to avoid giving answers to some of these questions before analyzing them, even though it will appear that that is what I am doing. For to pick any one discipline, say psychology, as an example of all those that we think of as social sciences indicates already that there is something they all share in common. So let me suggest at least this much. What distinguishes any of the social sciences from the natural is already implied in the name. The social sciences concern themselves with human beings as social and societal creatures, where the natural sciences address themselves to the data of the physical world. The only problem here, then, is what do we do with biology? This too, of course, is concerned with something physical. But it is quite different, obviously, from heat, light, magnetism, climate, or the layers of the earth. You probably already know that there is a whole sub-discipline of biology known as animal behavior, humans included.

The so-called "social world" contains within it classifications of human beings as individuals, and human beings in groups. Classify them in terms of societies or cultures, and we are in sociology. Classify them in terms of racial or civilization traits, and we are in anthropology. The obvious overlap is always a matter of concern. We have at least some real difficulty distinguishing culture, civilization, and societal characteristics and structures with any real distinctiveness. And this is reflected in the difficulty of clearly distinguishing sociology from anthropology. At what I might call the outer edges, there is little confusion. Here, sociology is concerned with the forms of social groupings, how groups hold together, the role that a group plays in the development of its individual members, the role that beliefs, ideas, values, and knowledge play in social formation and *re*-formation. But for some odd reason, ritual and ceremony have become part of anthropology, as has the problems of race, racial characteristics and modes of worship. On the other hand, problems of the relationship among work, the individual and society become the subject of economics. The latter has other concerns as well, of course -- what constitutes money, how it is earned and spent, the fluctuations in the value of money, how local and global trade takes place, what form it takes, what balances and disbalances are created, how spending and earnings are balanced in different societies and what happens in either case. The abstractions of "money," "rates of exchange," "incomes," "expenditures," and such become quite concrete within the study of specific groups, societies and nations. But what is evident is that all of this takes place in a social or societal context. Without this, there would be no field of economics. But without society, there still would be a field of physics, chemistry, even biology.

These governing patterns are of such variety in modes, organization, distributions, that its distinctive claims are obviously justified. And yet, again, without social structures there would be no governmental instruments. Indeed, there would be no need for them. But the study of government falls to political science, and only peripherally, in terms of outcomes, is it considered part of sociology.

The most interesting of this litany of distinctions is that of the place of psychology. At the outset, for example, Freud's work appeared to concentrate on the individual, whose inherent, inborn traits that are always in conflict with one another, produce a behavior that appears to be universally common among all people. Yet within his analyses, the social does appear as a powerfully determining factor in the struggle among the id, the ego and the superego. What then appears to begin as a study that focuses attention on intrinsic human behaviors moves quickly into the realms of societal sciences. Psychology borders now on anthropology. Further, with the developments of criticism of Freudian assumptions, a frankly social psychology appears in the works of George Mead, Clark Hull, William James, John Dewey, and Gordon Allport. Now human behavior is studied as completely determined by the structures and behaviors of societal groupings and societal beliefs, and how individual behavior in turn determines societal patterns of knowledge and behavior.

Yet while all this is going on, a wholly new approach is developed -- that of treating the individual as a biological mechanism where societal structures play only the external role of agents of stimulation, reward and punishment. Such activities may motivate behavior, but the behavior itself is a matter of the conditions of the electro-chemical-biological structure within the organism. As a result, this particular school of psychology moves out of the social sciences and much closer to physics and biology than sociology and anthropology where the earlier psychology is.

As for history, without exception, this is a field of study assigned to the social sciences. Except for the factor which I have already given some attention to, the factor of evidence being always of the past, this identification is unexceptionable. History is, after all, agreed upon as the study of human beings, as groups, cultures, civilization, nations, in terms of human, individual experiences, thoughts, beliefs, levels of knowledge, inventions and the ways in which experiences and decisions determine later conditions in the lives of people and societies. But in each of the others of the social sciences, the data dealt with is present data that can be examined, studied, experimented with now the present. As I have said, however, in history the evidence may be in the present but what the evidence is about cannot be. On that basis, we do find that sometimes history is listed among the Humanities Departments (along with the arts) and not with the social sciences.

Now, not all of this distribution and association is particularly confusing. At least in terms of the matters being studied, there is assuredly a justification for collecting them all under the title of "social sciences." But what of other distinctions that are not difficult to identify? Is there, for example, a common methodology among all of the social sciences, as there appears to be a common matter, distinguished only by emphasis on one or another facet of this common subject matter? Or are there genuinely different models and models required by each different facet? For example, is a model of society applicable to a model of economy? Will a model of societal behavior for purposes of explanation also serve as a model of individual behavior for the same purposes? And if, as I have said, methods of inquiry derive from models and metaphors, from models of thinking manifest in models and metaphors, and models differ among them, can there be a common methodology? But we know that in colleges everywhere there are courses called "The Methodology of the Social Sciences." So what's all the noise about? Why make such a big deal of it?

Only this: this book has the aim of teaching you how to think. If each discipline demands its distinctive model, we had better know and learn it. If not, we might find ourselves thinking, for instance, like physicists when we should be learning the thinking processes of historians, psychologists, or sociologists. The ensuing confusions would be horrendous.

Let us get into the details of this matter a little more carefully. Now, I will not go through each of the above mentioned disciplines, but I can offer some general contrasts by focusing primarily on what is called social psychology. If I were to offer an analogy, first, in order to distinguish between this and behaviorism or positivist psychology, as it is sometimes called, I would say that in the one case trees are studied in the context of a total environment, seeing its "behavior" as determined partly by its inner organization of elements and parts, but also to some degree by the conditions of soil, water, availability of sunlight and air. In the other, attention is paid exclusively to the inner structure alone, considering the external influences only as stimulants and nourishment. Put another way, the first is called a synthetic approach; the second, an analytical approach. The first seeks a synthesis of all possible influences in growth and behavioral changes; the second analyzes the self-sustaining structure of a thing or a system.

The difference here then is a difference between two views of the human being whose behaviors are being explained. In comparing psychology with other disciplines, something rather different becomes apparent. Other disciplines are concerned, obviously, with other facets or dimensions of individual and societal behaviors. But between the two we cover a wider arena of problems. On the one hand we want to find out why a single discipline uses such different models and offers such different explanations. On the other, on what basis do we assume that all these different disciplines are classed within a singular, functional system for exploring, explaining, and describing -- matters which if not very diverse are still different enough to justify classification into those other disciplines?

First, we need to examine this concept of a single discipline that offers such different explanatory models and uses such different root metaphors. Is it really a single discipline? In terms of the matter under inquiry, is it really one discipline, perhaps seen in several ways? Or is it several distinct disciplines after all? If we argue from the view of method, as a distinguishing criterion for identification of a discipline, something else must be taken into account here.

Throughout, I have been demonstrating that "method" is not simply a series of steps to be used for the resolution of either a puzzle or a problem. I have been showing that method derives from and is shaped by a model especially construct-ed for purposes of inquiry. The purpose of such a methodological model is to develop an explanation of something we seek to understand or understand better. Any model, then, must contain several things within it if the inquiry is to be fruitful. In order for all this to happen, the model must be a faithful depiction

It must also have built into it the metaphoric system from which the event is seen, or more correctly *seen as*. So, for example, a behaviorist model of psychology will reflect the notion that "man is a machine." Without such an inclusion we would only have a more or less faithful image of the event itself, and be as much at a loss about how to go about conducting or even beginning our inquiry as we are faced with the event to be studied. Thus, it is not simply the event that directs the making of the model; it is the primary or root metaphor that determines the form it will take, and the functions it is anticipated it has. If you want to see how this works, just consider making a model of the human who is "an element of nature, growing in the field of events which are the sources of continued growth." The machine model is not only inadequate now to describe and explain man, it is simply not a model of man. And if it is not, then anything that is said from the models is not said about human beings, but about machines with certain features that seem vaguely similar to those of a human being. Suppose you come upon a mechanical sculpture, that is, made of iron and chrome with wires and lights, but made in a human form. But your interest was trying to understand how a human being responds to sunsets and bird songs. However the sculpture, in external features, looks like a human, you would hardly expect to find any answers to your questions.

How does this relate to the questions of the identity of psychology as a discipline? In one sense, all too obviously. In another, the analogy I suggest may need further tinkering with in order to make it more complete and more apt. What is being suggested is that a model must take into account just what the metaphor places its emphasis upon. And that a rejection of a metaphor is not so much based on its failure to take reality into account as on the fact that it fails to take account of a prevailing metaphor. So to argue that man is more than just a machine is, by implication, that man is seen as something else, derived from some other root metaphor.

Thus, the schools of psychology, with their different models are saying, each of them, that "human beings are not what you say they are. They are something (someone?) else. Therefore, the behavior of people is to be explained in this way, in these terms, not in your way or in your terms." So humans become many different things, as many as there are different schools of psychology. And all the rest of us are left wondering, "Yes, but what are humans, really?" The suggestion to look at humans, look at them without presupposition, without premeditation, with clear and innocent eyes is mythical, after all. There are simply no such eyes. We see what we have learned to see. We see humans only "*as* ...."

So the problem, and it is one when there is dispute, is not resolved by just taking another look at the thing being modelled. It is resolved through argument, through analysis of competing models, and finally through an evaluation of the conflicting metaphors given body in those models. Now this does not happen very often, I suspect, because the idea of metaphoric basis for a model may be some kind of embarrassment to tough-mined scientists or scholars. Besides, it deprives any model of its claim to reflect only the hard realities of things. It makes the whole affair, the whole discipline, such an arbitrary business, and yet, any debate over what man is, or is like, is just such an argument.

When an argument develops over what are to be considered the essential traits to be included in a model, over what does and what does not enter into a definition of humans, we are in regions where innocent observation makes no contribution. What do such eyes tell us, for example, of proclivities? What does a proclivity look like? What appearance does it have or make? Has it color? Dimension? Form? The very question is loaded, you see. For if you say it has none of these, then the person who has asked it adds, "Well, if it has none, why try to include it in your model? Why put in a symbol of something that has no tangible existence in the first place?" The metaphor has already been implied: in that model, the symbols represent only tangible, observable things and events. To include anything else is to include mythological figments which direct attention away from what is *really* there.

On the other hand, to hold for a metaphor or a total, interdependent environment leads to alternative conceptions of reality. Here a proclivity is not a present and measurable event. It is a relationship between events that are determinate, though it is not itself determinate or measurable. "Motivation" is real, though not in the same way "actuality" is real. "Tendency" is not a thing. It is a logical implication which, when dismissed, reduces explanation by eliminating much that is implicit because it has not yet become an actuality. "Mind" is dismissed as anything other than tangible brain function. What of a "tragic sense of life"? How would one account for "reverence" when one hears the organ in a church playing "Ave Maria"? How can you possibly dismiss it as mythic, as you have dismissed "freedom" and "dignity"? Is not this too an essential, defining quality of humans? How is this to be explained? It does not have to be explained, say the mechanistic (behavioral) model. It cannot quantify "reverence" just as it cannot quantify "dignity" or "freedom."

And there you have it -- the irresolvable dispute. Except for one thing. Consequences. Psychologists do have agreements on many matters of behavior. No one denies that some behavior is coherent and others incoherent. Some behavior shows a "reality" orientation and others, like the delightful story of a seven foot rabbit in *Harvey*, a "reality disorientation." Rational and irrational behaviors are observable. Whatever explanations can we offer to account for these? Whatever name you give to certain behaviors, the behavior itself has to be confronted. If, from your model, you have been able to explain it, I must pay attention, even though I may think you have done something you are not able to explain in your terms, in your model. What you have done works, but not as well as with my model.

I had earlier pointed out that it appears to be a scandal that in their professional meetings psychologists cannot come to agreement over what their discipline addresses itself to, what methods will be employed, and what models will be the source of those methods. But when we consider this matter of borrowing from whatever models are available, have shown some evidence of achievement, perhaps, it is not such a scandalous state of affairs after all. What discipline has ever come into existence full blown, complete, needing no further development? None that I can think of, with the possible exceptions of the geometry of Euclid and the logic of Aristotle (like Athena, springing full grown and complete in her wisdom from the head of Zeus -- what a marvelous metaphor!). Only many centuries later did new growth occur, resulting in non-Euclidian geometry and symbolic or linguistic logics. In so complex and beguiling a problem as humans present, can we expect anything but complicated arguments over definition, function, determinate traits? The so-called scandal, then, is nothing more than the scandal that it took so long for the debates to get under way. Why was it not started in the 4th Century? The 7th? The 13th? Why did it take until the 19th Century to finally face the issue? Like Euclid's conception of geometry, the primary metaphors for humans had powerful publicity agents at work and controlled 99.9% of it. Now the dialogue is on, the contests have been joined. Psychiatrists freely borrow from psychoanalysts, and vice versa. Behaviorism, once completely analytical, now borrows from social psychology matters to be put under logical analysis, as part of the "inner" structures of the behavior. And social psychologists borrow the methods of the clinically oriented psychologists.

The models that a discipline begins with at the outset of its career are, to be sure, vital to the form and the achievements of that discipline. But the models that develop from debate, analysis, further explorations and experiments are demonstration of the vital character of a discipline. Any particular individual of a discipline may be persuaded that s/he is the new Athena, but no individual constitutes the whole of the discipline. Euclid is not all of geometry; Aristotle is not all of logic; Freud is not all of psychology; Einstein, not all of physics. Indeed, the presence of such awesome monuments of intelligence makes them finally the icons against whom rebellions and therefore new growth can take place. They become the orthodoxies that appear to make alternatives a promise or chaos. Conversely, if members have all agreed on one set of models from which all knowledge will spring, if no argument can ensue, if no growth can occur, then the very vitality of that discipline dissipates and it becomes moribund. What then of psychology? Does it have a single face? A single focus? Is it a singular discipline? Not yet. In intention, at least. If these answers properly reflect one state of affairs, then it ought to be taught as a discipline seeking identity, and studied as just that. As it is, it is taught, all too often, as sets of competing dogmas in which every other view is a considered "false dogma."

I cannot resist the temptation of looking at education for a moment to demonstrate just this idea. Walk around your high school or college and ask your teachers how they know that learning has gone on and you will discover some pretty diverse models in use. One teacher will tell you that students should "develop" in his/her class (a biological model based on a growth metaphor); another will tell you that the purpose of teaching is to increase the cognitive structure (a mind model based on interconnecting circuits); another will tell you that s/he provides input that the student processes (obviously, a computer model); and still another will frankly tell you that they cannot be concerned with what happens in the brain or the mind, only what behavior the students exhibit (a behaviorist model, currently in vogue through the work of Madeline Hunter). All these demonstrate that the competition that exist in the schools of psychology have a corresponding effect on how we perceive the learning process.

But why include psychology among the social sciences? Should it be classified there? Again, what and where it is now is probably not what and where it will be later. At one time, in Paris, psychology was identified with the field of literature since Freud used so much of Greek mythology as the sources of his metaphors and its models. Then it moved into the social sciences because of the work of James and Mead; then into the natural sciences because of Watson, Pavlov, and Skinner. Its later association is now being formed, though we may not yet be in a position to predict what it will be. Nevertheless, the discussions here, under the aegis of the social sciences, have value because it represents too what occurs in the whole domain of what I have called the mixed model realm of explanation. Economics, sociology, anthropology, political theory, are very much in the same state. Indeed, not only these specific disciplines, but the whole arena called the "social sciences" is in a state of action, moving toward a firmer definition of itself. If the natural (physical) sciences seem to have achieved a more definitive form, it is simply a demonstration that the tangible world of things is less complex than people and societies are. And yet, it is becoming evident that the natural sciences are less definitive than they were a hundred years ago. Earlier, universally accepted models and metaphors through which, within which the natural sciences produced their explanations of nature and nature's way, are inexorably leading to the development of newer models, and these sciences now appear as much in a state of confusion and dispute as are the social sciences. The tendency of some social sciences to become like the natural sciences is being accompanied by a reverse movement. The natural sciences are apparently moving toward the social sciences. That is a rather astonishing turn of events. The sciences which have developed nuclear power and with it nuclear bombs, now find it necessary to include in their concerns, the conditions of human, social existence and the moral implications of their research.

Nevertheless, at any given time, we do not have the luxury of waiting for what yet will develop in a particular discipline. All of us, scholars, experimenters, teachers and students must become part of the process of its development and contribute to its growth. The fault -- if it is a fault -- is with each of us who consider a discipline at any moment as the reservoir of knowledge to be distributed and learned, nothing more. If we see it always as a discipline "in the making," as a model-making activity in which newer models are constantly being made, then we become part of the mainstream of activities from which new instruments of analysis, exploration and explanation are constantly being formed. Now, such an appeal runs counter to our ordinary expectations as students. We come to school all prepared to learn what is presented to us, to absorb the knowledge our betters place before us. If they do not have such knowledge, what are they doing there in the front of the classroom? Why are they getting paid? Why are we doing the paying, when we are both involved in the activity of reshaping an existing discipline and inventing more promising models? A good question, and one I do not intend to answer in any great detail, except to offer these. Maybe it is because model-making itself has to be taught. Maybe, before we do begin to make models of greater effectiveness, we ought to know what models have already been invented and used, and what outcomes have been produced by them. If we now recognize the tentative status of models and the constant need to remake them, this does not eliminate the necessity of learning what has already been constructed and what has already been explained as a result.

But from this consideration of the problems within a given discipline, let us turn to the other question of why several seemingly distinct disciplines are classified under a single organizing title.

We recognize that to treat a society as a single person is an example of an unconsciously misused metonymy; the whole ascribed the quality or characteristics and functions of a part. Or an unguarded pathetic fallacy, unguarded because it is treated literally. Society is not an individual. Its collectiveness is only a logical ascription, not an actuality, and must not be treated as such. "Society" does not speak. Some members of that society do speak, not for society, but for individuals who in small or large groups have come to some kind of agreement that is now being announced. To say that it is "society" which speaks is to cover up the data, and make response or challenge difficult, if not dangerously heretical. Who or what do we address when we answer "society"?

Nevertheless, the classification of "social" as in the social sciences is not empty. Clearly, it has as its references all those "sciences" whose concern in a group of different activities is common either in substance or in process. In this case, it is to be assumed, it is a common substance, each specific discipline addresses itself to. Each, as I have said, is concerned with some facet of society or social living: as organization, in its origins, its economies, its governance, and so on, along with the behaviors of its members of the social group. The real problem was, you may remember, that of trying to find a methodology that all the distinctive disciplines might share. And that calls for further scrutiny.

We have all of us been introduced to the "scientific method" at some time in our education. This method has been distilled in this way: a problem appears to us as a disruption or an arrest of normal, ongoing activity. Our first concern, then, is to identify and/or locate what has prevented a normal activity from proceeding normally. We examine the details of the given activity to see if we can locate the event or the sudden cessation of function of a specific part of the event that has arrested or distorted the whole of the ongoing activity. After observation of this we offer a hypothesis of what needs to be done to remove the obstruction or repair the element whose functioning has ceased. This hypothesis is the directive for the next action for the performance of an experiment which recommends we do certain things to restore the action. If the disrupted activity now begins, starts up again, then the first hypothesis has been appropriate. We restate the hypothesis again in the form of a statement that when such and such happens, the following is to be done. The problem is solved. We have used the "scientific method" properly and effectively. The model of proper functioning is adequate and the operation is back at work.

If generalized enough and if proper translations are made so that the terms of the method can be made to apply equally to human affairs, behaviors and disruptions as they seem to apply to the inanimate things of nature, then the method can be said to apply equally in the social as well as the natural sciences. And if that is the case, then the resolution of societal or social problems of whatever kind are similar to the problems in the physical world, at least methodologically. And "science" is a term that both sets of disciplines can use. Not only that, but as this method of resolution of problems is refined in the physical domain, its improvements ought to be equally applicable to that other domain, the social.

There's the rub: can it? Are the problems of humans and societies similar in character to physical problems? Can the method used for explaining meteorological changes also be applied to changes in the emotional states of people? Can a model of cloud formation, temperature changes, wind direction, wind velocity, heat sources, modes of cooling and models of rising temperatures also be read as measuring, following, explaining the changes in the "heat" or "coldness" of feelings which we identify as "emotional states"? Is a person weeping to be understood as "clouds condensing into water"? Do we intend this to be a literal description or metaphoric? I think few of us would doubt that the expression is a metaphor, and not a literal statement claiming identity between the two. But do economists, sociologists, or anthropologists see this as metaphoric? I suggest that this is something that you ought to find out for yourselves in some of your classes. I have indicated that at least one school of psychology rejects the whole idea that science can grow or perform its functions on the basis of metaphor. Behaviorists have argued that one of the requirements of psychological science is to replace every metaphor with a literal statement, every theory with a statement of fact. This is to be done by establishing equivalences between tangibles. And to do this, it is best to eliminate all statements that do not refer to literal actualities. Is this also done in the other members of the social sciences? If it is, we have what Auguste Comte, the 19th Century sociologist, has called "positive" science. We only talk of what is, tangibly, and talk about it in exact, literal terms. If we cannot locate an equivalence in humans of "temper" changes, then let us only talk about rain in its terms, and weeping in its own terms, and stop all this talk about them either as equivalences or as metaphors. Talk only about them in terms that refer to actualities and treat them as distinctive manifestations of nature, one physical, the other human. Do not claim for one what you claim for the other, unless you can demonstrate identity.

Nevertheless, it can be pointed out that other social scientists offer their explanatory statements in literal terms, would resist any assertion that what they say is metaphorically based, but do not go as far as the positivists do. Those who do, I must admit, are refreshing. Those who openly admit to the metaphoric basis and status of their arguments and explanations provide me, at least, with a sense of relief that comes from a promise of someone who is able to change their minds.

But let us come back to our basic questions. What is scientific about the social sciences? And on what basis are the social sciences grouped together? To put it more bluntly, on the basis of a broader conception of science as a method, and on the recognition that however distinctive may be the particular methods of each of the "social" disciplines, they have a common process in some broader conception of scientific methodology.

I suggest this broader conception of that process of thinking we call scientific can be derived from the idea that whatever else a discipline may be doing (as I have described above) it does so by being concerned to create models of inquiry into events being studied.   Descriptions and explanations, hypotheses and observations are capable of being invented at any given moment. New situations, then, are explored in the terms of the models we have learned to use, with some degree of skill. But in the use, not only are we able or unable to solve problems, but the very models themselves are being tested and evaluated -- not only for their applicability in given situations, but for what they allow us to see -- the problems they allow us to resolve. If we do more than give lip service to the notion that science is method, then we will hold more firmly to the implied notion that science develops as "better" methods develop. This will not occur unless we pay attention, not to outcomes, but to the methods themselves, to their characteristic processes, their forms, what they are predicated on, as well as what visions are part of them, what outcomes they make available and, even more important, what they limit us to and what alternative models become apparent in the very act of using those we have at hand.

In this sense, all sciences are members of the same family, whether natural or social.   Moreover, the statement about the way models of inquiry are constructed and employed does not require the translation of data into tangibles. Models themselves are tangible, whether they are representative or analogical. If they are representative, they are selective presentations of actual data. If they are analogical, they are tangible manifestations of intangibles. Error is avoided in the simple assertions that one cannot analyze something in any literal sense, and that my analysis must begin with the simple notion that "I am considering this or that as ...." If you disagree, then tell me how you see this? What are you considering this to be *as*? I look at light as fluids in motion. Do you prefer to see it as the behavior of particles, pellets shot from a gun? Fine. What does this permit you to say about light that my perspective does not? I see society as a many-headed creature, but all of whose voices are one voice. Fine. You may say you do not view society this way, but as many individuals whose many voices argue with each other, but who, when they speak, never speak as one, but as groups of voices, as in a choral society. The tenors say this. The altos say that. And the basses say yet another thing.

See how the metaphors, even contrasting ones, provide richer and greater explanations than the simple statement of "this society holds this particular view"?

Now apply this concept of methodology of science to sociology, anthropology, economics, of political theory. Are their methods common? Do their conclusions have a scientific status seen in the terms described in the paragraph above? Is anything to be gained by learning to think in what is now identified as thinking as a social scientist? If not, then we have clarified the merit of a claim, negatively. If so, then the thinking processes of each of the members of the group classified here should be better understood, open to a better model of critical analysis, its claims better understood as, at best, always being tentative, awaiting a more fruitful metaphor waiting to be invented. And although each of these disciplines may be different as particulars, they perform as forms of explanation in the same way.

There is, I must point out, a special function that metaphor plays in the social sciences (and in history, too), that it does not in the natural sciences. This is the function of creating empathy for experimenter and student alike. Where feeling states play a role in the conduct of human beings, and we are seeking to understand how those feelings affect choice and action, it is only by means of well-chosen metaphors that those feelings may be brought into a present exploration. An intimacy is created between past and present; between the distant and the nearby. For as we share a world with others when we share commitment, so a common metaphor, so we share an experience across continents or across the ages. The Irish have often considered themselves the "Blacks of Europe"; the Japanese have sometimes called themselves the "Jews of the ancestral world." Some blacks have argued that no one but an African American can know the rejection and the defiling of one of their own. All I can say is, what little imagination this shows. Every group, every member of a religion has, in its history, experienced rejection, has known what it is to be reviled, scorned, murdered, just for being -- Black, Jewish, Christian, Armenian, Irish, B'hai, Sunic, Shiite, and on and on. It is evidence of withdrawal from the world, from thinking itself, to see only this person, this race, this society, as experiencing terror. Anthropologists, for example, who fail to use metaphor for the achievement of intimacy between themselves and the subjects studied, very simply, do a bad job. Read some of the works of Margaret Mead as a marvelous example of a researcher who has used metaphor to create the bond of intimacy that brings with it the confidence needed to learn what she sought to learn. If this is also an elemental function which appears in the arts, too, it is nevertheless fundamental in the social sciences as well. Without it, these sciences are only statistical tables. Variability of behavior and choices go ostensibly un-understood or not taken into account at all. And poll-takers are always being surprised that actual results rarely, if ever, square with what their polls had predicted. Such intimacy has no place in the physical sciences. Molecules do not withhold agreement when magnetic forces are present. Nor can water refuse to rise to its own level because it finds earth immoral. To seek to empathize with molecules and the flow of water is a form of pathetic fallacy that only fabulists, poets, and other madmen would use. But when the subjects of study are human beings, past or present, no other way to reach across time and place is available to us. If sometimes we may be misled by analogy, at times, in such a quest; if sometimes, too, many claims are made by means of this function of metaphor, it is not because of the metaphor, but because of a particular one that we have chosen. We are warned by anthropologists to be extremely careful not to read present meanings and present powers backwards into the past, or sideways, onto other cultures. And this to be sure is sound advice. But such advice, followed blindly, denies us any access whatever to distant or alien cultures or people. The more that the details of both sides of these analogies of feelings show similarities, the greater the possibilities of appreciating how those feelings have affected choice, and modes of response. To say it is impossible to understand another people or another culture is to say I have found no adequate analogy, because the worlds are too different from mine. How sad, especially for a scholar, this absence of thought and imagination. How unfortunate to have been dominated by a model that isolates every individual from every individual, every culture from every culture, every society from every society, leaving each of them alone in a world without connecting lines of thought. And how amazed we are when we read reports of other groups -- and discover that they are not just like us, they *are* us. The Japanese have said how astonishing that a Jew (Sholom Aleichem) could know so much about the Japanese that he could write a story, transformed into a musical drama called *Fiddler on the Roof*.

Some Final Thoughts

Rather than offer some conclusions to this long chapter, let me address a concern that students will often voice as they reach the close of a course or book such as this. It deals with an attitude that some will come to have about learning how to think, and the attitude that may jade your experiences as you enter your years at college.

There is sometimes the tendency to become rather cynical when one finds out that what they thought was real was only a ruse, a deception, a means of pulling the wool over one's eyes. If you have, at the end of this work, adopted a little of this cynicism, then that is unfortunate. Its intention, you will remember, was not to produce cynicism, but to develop your powers of thinking, to show you "how the world goes" through the construction of models and metaphors. This book has been about the difference between the experiences of our existence and our attempts, however meager or however grand, to make sense of those experiences.

As stated early in Chapter 2, the professors you will encounter in college are, by and large, reasonable and honorable people. Their purpose is to show you how the world can be viewed through the particular disciplines in which they hold membership. What has been lacking among all these courses you have learned and will be learning is a cohesive foundation to see how the world has been reconstituted in the form of models of description, of explanation, of inquiry and of expression. In this sense, there is no chicanery involved; there is only honest portrayal of the world as seem through the eyes of that discipline.

If you finally subscribe to my thesis and have been convinced by its arguments, you will be able to approach all your studies with a new sense of wonder. You will look for the models and metaphors within each new piece of knowledge you encounter. You will recognize conventions for what they are, the agreed upon views and rules for living in the world. You will see poetry in a different light as you explore the imagery produced by the skillful manipulation of oxymoron, pathetic fallacy, and so on. Art will take on a new meaning, since you will try to establish how the artist celebrates the inner world of laughter, of love or torment through the combination of brush strokes, shapes and color. In the sciences, you will no longer confuse the models with what the models are designed to represent. You will see "atoms" as metaphors that allow us to envision something we may never be able to see. Your histories will be richer as you realize that the one historical model you learned is just that, only one model, to explain the long course of human events.

What then the attitude? I suspect that you can become again as you were years ago when you played with blocks. You spent hours constructing, arranging, taking apart, rearranging, reconstructing those items into whatever configuration that you fancied. And learning and thinking are just that way: not as sources of cynicism and arrogant pride, but as just another means of play; to enjoy some downright fun.

REFERENCES

Allport, Gordon. (1981). *Personality and Social Encounter: Selected Essays.* Chicago: University of Chicago Press.

Black, Max. (1962). *Models and Metaphors.* Ithaca: Cornell University Press.

Belth, Marc. (1965). *Education as a Discipline.* Boston: Allyn and Bacon, Inc.

Belth, Marc. (1970). *The New World of Education.* Boston: Allyn and Bacon, Inc.

Belth, Marc. (1977). *The Process of Thinking.* New York: David McKay Company, Inc.

Campbell, Norman. (1953). *What is Science?* New York: Dover Publications, Inc.

Dewey, John. (1933). *How We Think.* Lexington, MA: D.C. Heath and Company.

Duncan, Ronald and Miranda W. Smith. (1979). *Encyclopedia of Ignorance.* Greenville, NC: Wallaby Press.

Gregory, Richard. (1981). *Mind in Science: A History of Explanations in Psychology and Physics.* London: Cambridge University Press.

Hanson, N.R. [S. Toulminland and H.Woolf, Editors] (1971). *What I Do Not Believe, and Other Essays.* Norwell, MA: Kluwer Academy.

Hesse, Mary. (1966). *Models and Analogies in Science.* Notre Dame, IN: University of Notre Dame Press.

Hobhouse, Henry. (1986). *Seeds of Change.* New York: Harper & Row Publishers.

Hofstadter, Douglas. (1989). *An Eternal Golden Braids.* New York: Random House.

Hull, Clark. (1974). *Essentials of Behavior.* Westport, CT: Greenwood Press.

James, William. (1955). *Pragmatism.* Cleveland: Meridian.

Kuhn, Thomas S. (1962). *The Structure of Scientific Revolutions.* Chicago: The University of Chicago Press.

Lakoff, George and Mark Johnson. (1980). *Metaphors We Live By.* Chicago: The University of Chicago Press.

Langer, Suzzane. (1951). *Philosophy in a New Key.* New York: Mentor.

Mead, George H. [A. Strauss, Editor] (1964). *George Herbert Mead on Social Psychology.* Chicago: University of Chicago Press.

Popper, Karl R. (1968). *The Logic of Scientific Discovery.* New York: Harper and Row, Publishers.

Rescher, Nicholas. (1964). *Hypothetical Reasoning.* Amsterdam: North Holland.

Ricoeur, Paul, et al. (1984). *Time and Narrative, Volume I.* Chicago: The University of Chicago Press.

Ryle, Gilbert. (1955). *Concept of Mind.* London: Hutchinson's University Library.

Skinner, B. F. (1972). *Beyond Freedom and Dignity.* New York: Bantam Books.

Turbayne, Colin Murray. (1962). *The Myth of Metaphor* (revised). Columbia: University of South Carolina Press.

INDEX

About the Author:

Marc Belth received his Ph.D. from Columbia University and was Professor of Philosophy of Education at City University of New York at Queens College from 1951 until 1977. He taught or lectured at dozens of universities and colleges throughout the United States, Canada and England. He conducted two very successful radio lecture series in New York and was a consultant to the Canadian Teachers Federation Commission on Teacher Education. His Belth Centré at the Point Grey School in Vancouver, British Columbia, was a project to incorporate his educational principles into eighth grade classrooms. He was the author of *Education as a Discipline* (1965), *The New World of Education* (1970), and *Process of Thinking* (1977).

About the Editor:

Gerard T. Johansen received his M.S. in Education from Queens College in 1972 and has taught in several schools in New York State. He helped design and conduct a major research project, through Cornell University, in upstate New York public schools and has been a consultant to the New York State Education Department. He is currently a teacher at John Jay High School, Katonah-Lewisboro Schools, where he offers to college-bound students a semester course that is based on *Metaphor and Thinking: The College Experience.*